CROWN AND PEOPLE

CROWN AND PEOPLE

Philip Ziegler

COLLINS
St James's Place, London
1978

William Collins Sons & Co Ltd
London · Glasgow · Sydney · Auckland
Toronto · Johannesburg

First published 1978
© Philip Ziegler 1978

ISBN 0 00 211373 2

Set in Monotype Baskerville
Made and Printed in Great Britain by
William Collins Sons & Co Ltd Glasgow

Contents

Illustration Credits

Acknowledgements

Tom Harrisson, creator of Mass Observation, should have written this book. He had planned to do so after completing *Living Through the Blitz*, but had done no more than jot down a few notes when at the beginning of 1976 he was tragically killed in an accident in Bangkok. Without his dynamism and creative imagination this book would never, could never have been written.

The Trustees of the Mass Observation Archive have given me every assistance in my work. In particular Professor David Pocock has been the source of invaluable encouragement and advice. Mrs Dorothy Wainwright, Secretary of the Archive, was invariably helpful. Without her the Survey of the 1977 Jubilee could never have been organized. I also would like to thank by name all those who over the years have contributed to the treasure house of material now accumulated at the University of Sussex, but the Mass Observers have made anonymity a condition of their co-operation and it would be wrong to breach the rule. To all of them, past and present, both I and future students owe a great debt of gratitude. Mr William Hamilton, MP, has most generously allowed me to read the massive collection of letters which he has accumulated over the years and to quote freely from them. Miss Mollie Tarrant has guided me through the intricacies of Mass Observation and helped immeasurably in giving this book whatever scientific credibility it possesses. The work which Mr Leonard Harris did and commissioned for his book *Long to Reign Over Us?* has proved of singular value. Among those others who have assisted in various ways are Sir Alan Lascelles, Mr Bryan Bates of the British Market Research Bureau, Mr Andrew

Acknowledgements

Best, Mr Reg Gadney, Mr John O'Brien of National Opinion Polls Ltd, Professor Richard Rose of the University of Strathclyde, Mr Humphrey Spender and Mr J. Stevenson. Mr Richard Cohen, my editor, has contributed much useful and salutary advice. To all these my thanks.

My wife and children have endured a far more thorough immersion in royal affairs than they ever expected to be their lot. In particular they had a testing time during the celebration of the Silver Jubilee. For their forbearance and help I am truly grateful.

Preface

Those who write about the British monarchy, even the professional historians amongst them, are apt to generalize with some confidence about the feelings of the people towards their sovereign. 'George IV was the most hated man in his kingdom'; 'There was hardly a dry eye in the country when the old King died' – such observations, at varying levels of sophistication, punctuate the pages of the most sober narratives. Their authors may be right. Probably they are not far wrong. But the one thing quite certain is that *they do not know*. For until shortly before the 1939 war virtually no attempt had ever been made to find out what the British people felt about any of the social issues of the day. Parliamentary elections, of course, allowed them to choose between different groups of politicians supporting different policies, but whether they preferred gardening to reading, believed in a life hereafter or felt that King Edward VIII should marry an American divorcée were issues on which their views were cloaked in mystery.

It was in part Mr Baldwin's conviction that he spoke for the British people on this final issue that in 1937 provoked Tom Harrisson, Charles Madge and some other like-minded people to set up Mass Observation. This organization, as well as conducting studies in depth in given areas, set out to establish a network of volunteer reporters throughout the country who would record what people said or did on selected dates and with relation to certain specified themes. Observers were also encouraged to keep diaries in which they were asked to pay special attention to selected aspects of their national life.

The monarchy was always a particular interest of Mass

Observation. The Coronation of 1937 was followed with care and the results of these researches incorporated in *July 1937*, a book published at the end of the same year. Diarists throughout the war made regular references to the role of the royal family. The death of King George VI and the Coronation of Queen Elizabeth II were made the subject of special studies. In 1965 a poll was commissioned on behalf of Mass Observation by Mr Leonard Harris and provided the framework of his book *Long To Reign Over Us?* In 1977, by which time Mass Observation as such existed only as a commercial entity, the original volunteer organization was revived to report on the celebration of the Jubilee.

Mass Observation has sometimes been derided as 'amateur' – 'a Dad's Army of amateur journalists and autobiographers scouring the country for "overheards"' was Jonathan Raban's slightly acid phrase. In the sense that the work has been done for love, for pure delight in discovery with no commercial end in mind, then 'amateur' is a description in which to take pride. Julian Huxley described the early work of Mass Observation as 'far more scientific than many so-called "scientific" studies'. The praise was perhaps not wholly unequivocal; it is debatable how far the word 'scientific' can properly be applied to *any* study intended to establish what human beings say and think, still less what they feel subconsciously. Certainly Mass Observation is ill-equipped to quantify with any attempt at precision the *numbers* of people who feel one thing rather than another. For this task the opinion polls that have proliferated over the last twenty years are far better qualified. But such polls prove inadequate if not misleading in any situation where that question dreaded by pollsters, 'What do you mean by . . .?' can legitimately be posed. Mass Observation may produce less clear-cut answers – indeed it is not intended to produce answers at all – yet it can aspire to a truth beyond that accessible to its more 'scientific' descendants. In the forty years of its existence many hundreds of Observers have recorded, as objectively and fully as they are able, what the people around them have been seeing and doing on a variety of issues. From their reports a picture emerges which may not be clear-cut or exact in quantitative terms but still is closer to that elusive concept 'What the people think' than that provided by any other source. For those interested I annex to this book the report on the first ten years of Mass Observation prepared by Tom Harrisson in 1947. It remains the best statement of the ideals and principles underlying the organization's work.

It is this body of material, now concentrated in the Mass Observation Archive at the University of Sussex, which provides the largest element in my book. It is, however, far from being the exclusive fount of information. The opinion polls which have flourished since the Second World War have made the monarchy a favourite subject of their enquiries. It is striking how far they have tended to reinforce statistically the conclusions to which Mass Observation already pointed. Autobiographies, biographies and histories all contribute evidence, as, of course, does the press. There have been many special studies of the monarchy by sociologists and other academics, most of which have appeared in the learned journals of their profession. I have been singularly fortunate in being able to study the massive post-bag of Mr William Hamilton, an extraordinary collection of letters reflecting every shade of opinion to be found among those who feel strongly enough about royalty to write about it to a Member of Parliament. These and other, lesser sources are indicated where necessary in the notes. But the heart of this book is the material provided over the last forty years by the Mass Observers.

Some definition of the term 'people' is needed. Intellectuals are people, yet they are certainly not 'The People'; one of the most difficult problems facing those who chart popular opinion is that those who are most articulate in expressing it are rarely typical of those whose views they profess to be expressing. The voice of the people rings down the ages, but the chime is muffled by a blanket of prejudice wrapped around it by those who make words their profession. Historians and chroniclers rarely mean to be propagandists, but those who put their ears to the keyhole of public opinion are apt to hear what they expect or want to hear. It was to break down this barrier, to record *vox populi* direct rather than through the medium of the literary man, that Mass Observation was set up.

However inadequately, it is this voice that I have sought to record in the pages that follow, the voice of the man in the street, of that creature traditionally beloved by lawyers, 'the man in the Clapham omnibus'. Record enough men in enough streets and it is surely not too extravagant to hope that something approximating to a national norm will eventually emerge? Certainly, the more external evidence I have been able to amass, the less reason I have found to doubt the essential validity of the procedures of Mass Observation.

By 'the man in the street' I mean men in the streets of the British Isles. The geographical spread of the Observers and their apportionment between city, town and village has not been left to chance and reflects as faithfully as could be contrived the balance of population within the country. Regional distinctions have been apparent from the start and on the whole have remained consistent throughout the period, though the growth of Scottish and to a lesser extent Welsh nationalism is a factor beginning to disturb the traditional patterns. The voices of Commonwealth citizens from overseas are sometimes to be heard but only as part of the national picture. I have not attempted any study of the attitudes of their countries towards the monarchy any more than I have tried to explain the mingled fascination and dismay found so often among the Americans or the prurient curiosity of the cheaper French and German newspapers. It would be a fascinating subject for study, but the views of non-British observers, even those from the old Commonwealth countries which still recognize Elizabeth II as Queen, are based on premises so very different from those in Britain itself that any attempt to compare them would be nugatory if not positively misleading.

I have seen my function as mainly editorial; to select and, where necessary, interpret the voices of others in such a way as to reflect the weight of opinion among them. I have sought to be wholly objective. Having no passionately-held convictions on the subject myself I have not found the task too difficult. For those, however, who seek to detect a bias in my work it is perhaps only fair that I should state my opinions. I am a moderate royalist: that is to say that in the circumstances of Britain today I believe that constitutional monarchy is the most satisfactory system of government. I hold no brief for the institution in other countries, and have some reservations about the extension of privilege and perquisites to the outer fringes of the royal family, but I feel that Queen Elizabeth does a difficult and valuable job with conscientiousness, grace and good humour. That she lives in luxury seems to me obvious; that she ought to, equally so; I would not exchange my life for hers. At the risk of anticipating the conclusions that the reader may draw for himself at the end of this book, I may say that in this temperate approval of the monarchy I seem to reflect the opinion of the largest section of the British people.

CHAPTER ONE

The Crown in History

The concept of kingship, in one form or another, is as old as recorded history. Where then begin this book? It would be diverting and relatively easy to make a foray into *The Golden Bough*, trick out the fruits of the excursion with references to a few contemporary anthropologists, and end up with a heady brew of Homeric war-lords and Polynesian priest-kings. The relevance of such an exercise would, however, be as doubtful as the scholarship would be spurious. Even the hardiest savant would hesitate to establish too precise a relationship between the attitude towards his monarch shown by a Sumatran Iron-Age peasant and a Londoner today.

Fortunately there is no need to delve so deeply into the past or look so far afield to establish that kings were once held to be sacred and to possess miraculous powers. What Marc Bloch described as 'the whole group of superstitions and legends which form the "marvellous" element in the monarchical idea'[1] flourished in Britain in comparatively recent times. Nor were such beliefs confined to the less sophisticated parts of the community. James I claimed that 'kings are justly called Gods, because they exercise a manner of resemblance to Divine power on earth', and though his subjects were to reject his view within twenty years of his death it was none the less respectable intellectually. Robert Boyle, founder of the Royal Society and most eminent of seventeenth-century chemists, believed firmly in the royal touch as a cure for scrofula. Jeremy Collier, in his vastly learned *Ecclesiastical History of Great Britain,* as late as 1708 still took for granted the magical powers of the monarch: 'To dispute the matter of fact is to go to the excesses of scepticism, to deny our senses, and be incredulous even to ridiculousness.'[2] Henry IX, last 'king' of the Stuart line, was still touching against the Royal Evil as late as 1807. Even during the reign of Victoria gold coins bearing the portrait of the Queen were considered universal panaceas by some of the more backwoods inhabitants of Ross.[3]

Yet it is hard to accept that even the most credulous British peasant put much confidence in royal magic in the twentieth century, nor can it have been more than a quaint anachronism during the nineteenth. Somehow the force of the superstition had waned over the centuries, an erosion of belief which was both accelerated by political and social changes and also contributed to them. What Bloch describes as 'a deep-down shattering of faith in the supernatural character of royalty' had taken place as man evolved from the Dark Ages – now no longer considered so dark – to the equally questionable enlightenment of modern times.

Of course, even when this faith was still potent it rarely proved particularly efficacious if it clashed with the self-interest of the people.

> For God's sake let us sit upon the ground
> And tell sad stories of the death of kings:
> How some have been depos'd, some slain in war,
> Some haunted by the ghosts they have depos'd,
> Some poison'd by their wives, some sleeping kill'd,
> All murder'd—. . .

Richard II over-dramatized as usual, but the dismal roll-call of his peers goes far to prove his point. William I – died of injuries; William II – killed on the hunting-field, perhaps murdered; Stephen – fate obscure but almost certainly unpleasant; Richard I – killed in battle; John – hardly treated with respect; Henry III – defeated and imprisoned; Edward II – murdered; Edward III – died in desolate seclusion; Richard II himself – murdered; Henry VI – murdered; Edward V – murdered; Richard III – killed in battle: there were clearly limits to the reverence which the English felt towards their divinely anointed rulers. The Tudors managed things better, but the seventeenth century saw one king executed and another deposed. The Hanoverians survived because they conceded ever more effective power to their subjects and because it was convenient to the ruling élite that the institution of monarchy should be perpetuated. They rarely commanded the love of their people. What the British really felt about George IV is as little known as their views on any other subject, yet all the evidence there is suggests that he was the most detested man in his kingdom. With reason did *The Times* declaim: 'There never was an individual less regretted by his fellow-creatures than this deceased King.'

Yet something still remained. When Victoria succeeded to the throne she had on her side the advantages of youth and innocence; but even without such extras the position of the monarch was immensely strong. The habit of deference is not easy to shed. Herbert Spencer likened the submissive attitude shown by people in the presence of kings or princes to the 'fearful cringing' and pretence of being dead which our pre-human ancestors would adopt when confronted by superior and potentially hostile powers.[4] The reflection that the loss of one's estates or, worse still, one's head would be the likely consequence of incurring the royal displeasure must instil a certain timidity into one's attitude towards one's monarch. Though the Victorians had little reason to fear summary execution the Queen still disposed of enormous power; both in the bestowal of patronage and the punishment of misdeeds. For the rich and well-connected her displeasure could mean social ostracism; for the poor, victimization. To cower before her was not merely a vestige of traditional behaviour-patterns; it was a prudent precaution against disaster.

Even if it had not been so, however, the dwindling powers of the monarch would only gradually have been reflected in the reaction of the people. Ernest Jones illustrated how the shadow of power survived the substance by the story of a lady who visited a Canadian lunatic asylum and demanded by what right her husband was detained. Jones, who knew the doctor had perfectly good reasons, expected to hear him argue the case but instead he 'made a histrionic gesture and declaimed: "I do so in the name of the King."' The woman subsided, silenced if not satisfied. The King had no power over her, was wholly extraneous to her life, yet the invocation of his name was enough to quell her.[5]

But it was not by fear alone that the Queen commanded the respect of her subjects. 'A powerful, magnetic appeal exudes from the monarch,' wrote Max Weber, 'to which men are somehow peacefully and affectionately drawn.'[6] Because, before she returned to the cloisters after the death of Albert, she was generally seen in public in connection with some good work – opening a hospital, visiting a school – so the subconscious assumption was made that her presence was essential to the good work being performed: the hospital would not have been built without her stimulus, the school could never have run so smoothly but for her visit. As a quasi-deity she was dangerous but on the whole benevolent. The affection felt for her was rarely indeed based upon any personal experience; the loyalty of her subjects had wholly lost its traditional feudal basis of fealty offered in exchange for protection: yet neither the affection nor the loyalty were the less real for being hard to justify rationally. 'There is a world of unbought and uncalculated sentiment which matters vitally in politics . . .' wrote Ernest Barker. 'Reason has her sphere and her victories. Sentiment has also her triumphs and they are not the least noble . . .'[7]

Mankind has always needed grand and remote figures whom it can admire, perhaps even worship. Today the pop-star or football player to some extent supplies the need, but something less ephemeral is also called for. In the middle of the nineteenth century the monarch was virtually the only person who would have been readily recognized in every village of the land. The weight of stardom which was thus thrust upon the Queen was almost literally overwhelming. Society without her was inconceivable. 'Just as princesses cannot be abolished from fairy tales . . .,' wrote Ernest Jones, 'so it is impossible to abolish the idea of kingship in one form or another from the hearts of men. If people are emotionally starved in this way they invent sugar kings, railroad kings or magic "bosses".'[8] In the 1830s the possibilities for inventing surrogate monarchs were far less than in Britain today. Queen Victoria was as much part of popular mythology as Robin Hood or Father Christmas, yet enjoyed the decided advantage of being most evidently flesh and blood.

Yet though the Queen might have stepped out of a fairy story her role was not solely to satisfy the romantic urges of her subjects. For those concerned about the stability and security of the realm, for those who distrusted change or felt reforms should be carried out with due deliberation and respect for existing interests: the maintenance of the monarchy was of unique importance. 'His mere existence and his charisma,' wrote Weber of the constitutional monarch, 'guarantee the legitimacy of the existing social order.'[9] But though the monarch was the guarantor of the established order, it was important that he should never become the champion of the establishment. The peculiar strength of the monarchy, the reason why marriages with even the most estimable of subjects were deplored, was that it was free from faction, stood above every class of the community. In life-style the difference between the great landed aristocrat and the Queen might be insignificant; in spiritual or political consequence the gulf was immeasurable.

By its aloofness, its refusal to identify itself with any group of its subjects, the Crown preserved its freedom to act as a unifying force. It was nearly a hundred years after Victoria's accession that Lord Stamfordham described the function of the constitutional monarch. 'We must endeavour to induce the thinking working classes, Socialist and others, to regard the crown, not as a mere figure-head which, as they put it, "don't count", but as a living power for good, with receptive faculties welcoming information affecting the interests and social well-being of all classes, and ready, not only to sympathize with those questions, but anxious to further their solution.'[10] Victoria would have found the phraseology unfamiliar, would have been amazed and offended at the suggestion that anyone might consider she 'didn't count', yet she would have taken for granted the essence of Stamfordham's words. She was the Queen of the whole people: governments might come and go; reaction give way to reform and reform to reaction; she alone was constant.

The *New York Herald Tribune* was to refer, almost with irritation, to the way 'that no egalitarian American can understand, that the British crown binds together the British people'. Whether this unity was based on any real community of interests or whether it was spurious – a theatrical effect produced by trick lighting and judicious use of tinsel – is an issue on which neither historians nor sociologists can be expected to agree. What is certain is that the sentiment existed, that Britons felt the existence of some sort of link between themselves and Queen Victoria which could not have been justified by the objective facts of their relationship. 'The mysterious identification of king and people', wrote Jones, 'goes very far indeed and reaches deep into the unconscious mythology that lies behind all these complex relationships.'[11]

Harold Nicolson has vividly described the effect which Victoria must have had on her grandson, the young George V:

Even as a child Prince George must have noticed that in her presence those whom he himself feared or venerated became awestruck and diminished. The contrast between her personal homeliness and the majesty by which she was encompassed led him insensibly to look upon the Monarchy as something distinct from ordinary life, as something more ancient and durable than any political or family institution, as something sacramental, mystic and ordained.

Queen Victoria was by then a most formidable old lady, likely to intimidate the young and impressionable even without her royal status. Yet the young Victoria, by virtue of that status alone, could inspire awe and fear among men of far greater sophistication and experience than herself. Though George IV had degraded the currency and William IV done little to revalue it the monarchy was still an immensely potent factor in men's minds. It would have called for the most strenuous exertions on the part of Victoria to bring about a situation in which an announcement that the Queen of England was approaching would not have reduced any community to agitated turmoil, or the news of her unexpected death would not have caused, if not real grief, then at least profound disquiet throughout the country.

Victoria did make some such exertions, and the fact that the monarchy was in the long run even strengthened as a result is a tribute not so much to her wisdom as to the obstinate vitality of the institution. With the death of her husband, Albert, she withdrew into secluded grief and refused to perform those public functions which her people had grown to expect. What is the good of paying vast sums of money to support a Queen that we never see? asked critics of the Crown. The propensity of the Prince of Wales to become involved in scandal did not make matters easier. Under the leadership of Bradlaugh and Dilke the republican movement was rampant. Absentee Queen and libertine heir provided the matter for innumerable denunciations. By the early 1870s more than fifty republican clubs had been founded in different parts of Great Britain. At a huge rally in Hyde Park the Prince told his sisters, 'I hear some speakers openly spoke of a Republic . . . The Government really ought to have prevented it . . .'[12] He besought his mother to emerge from her sequestered gloom and show herself to the people:

> If you sometimes even came to London from Windsor – say for luncheon – and then drove for an hour in the Park and then returned to Windsor, the people would be overjoyed – beyond measure. It is all very well for Alix and me to drive in the Park – it does not have the same effect as when you do it; and I say thank God that is the case. We live in radical times and the more *the People see the Sovereign*, the better it is for the *People* and the *Country*.[13]

The Queen was not impressed. Demands that she should exhibit herself in public were unfeeling, disrespectful to the memory of her husband. Besides, the Prince's fears were nonsense: the times were not radical at all. When outrages were committed they were the work of a few fanatics: 'The country never was so *loyal* or so devoted to their Sovereign as now.'[14]

It was supposed to be the Prince of Wales's recovery from a dangerous illness which turned the tide of republicanism, but one may doubt whether that tide was running as strongly as it appeared to the alarmists. For behind the protests and the disaffection a new myth was forming, a myth which throve on the Queen's isolation and which perversely invested her with ever more romantic attraction as she dourly eschewed every romantic trimming:

> 'Ave you 'eard of the Widow at Windsor
> With a hairy great crown on 'er 'ead?
> She 'as ships on the foam – she 'as millions at 'ome,
> An' she pays us poor beggars in red . . .[15]

The image of this dumpy figure in mourning black, cooped up in her castle, mistress of a vast empire, mother and grandmother of Europe's royalty, immeasurably the most important woman in the world, caught the imagination of the people. It attained its apotheosis in that greatest of all imperial jamborees, the Diamond Jubilee, when from all over the world, in every variety of dress and uniform, princes and potentates poured in to pay homage to their monarch. All eye-witness accounts of her drive to a thanks-

'God save the Queen!'

giving service at St Paul's suggest that the Queen's own record of the occasion was in no way exaggerated:

> No one ever, I believe, has met with such an ovation as was given to me, passing through those six miles of streets . . . the crowds were quite indescribable, and their enthusiasm truly marvellous and deeply touching. The cheering was quite deafening, and every face seemed to be filled with real joy.[16]

They did not just respect and fear her; at that moment, at least, they loved her – loved her for her dowdiness, her obstinacy, loved her for the tears that streaked her face as she acknowledged their cheers. 'Go it, old girl!' called a voice from the crowd as she was pushed on to the Palace balcony in her wheel-chair, and the cry caught the authentic note of familiar affection which dominated the day.[17]

Those moments at which the adulation of the monarch is most intense are often marked by the sharp revulsion of those who distrust hero worship and prefer to stand aloof from popular rejoicings. The intellectual, the cynic and the natural rebel are usually to be found at times of coronation or royal wedding inveighing against the absurdity, the bad taste of such extravagant celebration. H. G. Wells, when a turbulent schoolboy, was representative of the malcontents, and in his first volume of autobiography wrote:

> For my own part, I heard too much of the dear Queen altogether, I conceived a jealous hatred for the abundant clothing, the magnificent housing and all the freedoms of her children and still more intensely of my contemporaries, her grandchildren . . . Various desperate and fatiguing expeditions to crowded street corners and points of vantage . . . from which we might see the dear Queen pass – 'She's coming. Oh, she's coming. If only I could see! Take off your hat Bertie dear' – deepened my hostility and wove a stout, ineradicable thread of republicanism into my resentful nature.[18]

Such outbursts, however, seem to have been rare. The traditional British passion for longevity ensured that the Grand Old Lady inevitably grew grander as she grew yet older. Buckingham Palace became the focal point for national rejoicing; the very fact that she went there so rarely meant that each visit became an occasion to be savoured. When Mafeking was relieved and it was known that the Queen was in town some 30,000 people massed outside the gates, sang songs and cheered loudly at her appearance. Three years later she died. If ever the cliché, 'the ending of an era',

had reality it was then. The Boer War had already killed
the first flush of imperial enthusiasm; the turn of the century
hinted at a new age of unparalleled progress; yet it was the
death of the old Queen which struck home to the people's
unconscious. Henry James, observing the scene with quizzi-
cal sympathy, noted that the streets seemed 'strange and
indescribable'. People were dazed and hushed almost as
though they were frightened – 'a very curious and un-
forgettable impression'.

It was a hard act to follow, and many doubted whether
Edward VII could do so. *The Times* gloomily reminded its
readers that the King had often been importuned by
temptation in 'its most seductive forms'. How often he must
have prayed 'lead us not into temptation', yet with a feeling
akin to hopelessness. This disrespectful attitude had become
a commonplace over the preceding decades. Edward had
begun his career with all the potential of a Prince Charming,
his gaiety and glamour an agreeable contrast to the sombre
dignity of the court. The rejoicing at his engagement to
the beautiful and sweet-natured Princess Alexandra showed
how starved the people had been of pageantry and popular
fiestas. A. J. Munby noted in his diary:

> The preparations for celebrating the Princess's arrival go
> on at a wondrous rate. Every house has its balcony of
> red-baize seats; wedding favours fill the shops, and flags
> of all sizes; often the banners are already waving, and the
> devices for illumination fixed . . . The town seems as full
> as in the height of the season: one may say that the car-
> penters and gas-fitters are all working day and night,
> while the rest of the population spend their time in watch-
> ing them.[19]

When the Danish princess arrived on 7 March huge
crowds gathered at Southwark and along the route taken
by her carriage. 'So many people were crammed between

the triumphal arches and the streaming banners that the police lost control of them in the city, and the Life Guards had to clear the way with drawn sabres.' As she passed Munby in King William Street, 'the populace, who had been rapidly warming to tinder-point, caught fire all at once. "Hats off!" shouted the men; "Here she is," cried the women; and all those thousands of souls rose at her, as it were, in one blaze of triumphant irrepressible enthusiasm, surging round the carriage; waving hats and kerchiefs, leaping up here and there and again to catch sight of her, and crying "Hurrah!" '

Metropolitan zest would not necessarily be reflected in other parts of the country. One of the problems in studying the relationship between monarch and people is deciding how far the hot-house atmosphere of the capital with its traditional passion for royal junketing would seem exaggerated and absurd in Leeds, Manchester or Glasgow. Windsor, crouching as it did in the shadow of the great castle, was little more typical than London of the country as a whole, and one cannot know whether the crowds that gathered around the railway station to see the royal couple off after the wedding would have been duplicated in any other town. Certainly few spectators would have been more obstreperous than the young Randolph Churchill. 'The policemen charged in a body, but they were knocked down. There was a chain put across the road but we broke that; several old *genteel* ladies tried to stop me, but I snapped my fingers in their face and cried "Hurrah!" and "What Larks!" I frightened some of them horribly.'[20]

Though the people's affection for Alexandra remained constant, the Prince of Wales's standing see-sawed wildly. His involvement in Lady Mordaunt's somewhat scabrous divorce case led to his being booed whenever he appeared in public. 'Even the staunchest supporters of monarchy shake their heads,' declared the popular newspaper, *Reynold's News*, 'and express anxiety as to whether the Queen's successor will have the tact and talent to keep royalty upon its legs and out of the gutter.' Then the Prince fell so ill that his life was despaired of. His recovery heralded an outburst of loyalty as extravagant as the earlier condemnation. The Queen emerged from her seclusion to take part in a procession of open carriages, waving to the crowd and from time to time kissing her son's hand. That evening the illuminated streets were packed. 'And amidst all this the working folk, men and women, boys and girls, merrily moving along, sometimes half a dozen lasses arm-in-arm, dancing in a row and singing, while the prentice swains danced by them, playing the flute or the accordion. I never saw such a crowd, nor a sight so striking in England . . .'[21]

So the fluctuations continued. In 1875, when money had to be raised for a royal tour of India, Bradlaugh told an angry crowd of 60,000 in Hyde Park that the nation did not want to stop 'the brave, moral, intellectual, future King of England' going to India. Indeed, they all hoped he would go a great deal farther, and stop there too; but not a penny for the jaunt should be found from public funds. The Tranby Croft scandal in 1891, when the Prince became involved in a case of cheating at baccarat in a country house and the papers revelled in exposing the dissolute life-style of their future king, produced a fresh wave of hostility. 'The monarchy almost is in danger,' Victoria told her daughter, 'if he is lowered and despised.' When the Queen died the popular mood was of doubt and fear for the future, yet it only took an attack of appendicitis and an emergency operation a few days before the scheduled date for the Coronation to swing sentiment back again. 'The Empire,' wrote Sir Philip Magnus excitably, 'was convulsed by a transport of emotional loyalty and of human affection for King Edward which commanded the awed sympathy and wonder of the world.'[22] It would be hard to produce chapter and verse in support of such hyperbole, but it was as likely to be true as the equally clamorous denunciation of the *Nottingham Express* at the time of Tranby Croft ten years before: 'The British Empire is humiliated and the rest of civilization is pointing a finger at us.'

The truth is that both points of view were held by wide sections of the population. Edward VII's finest hour was to come in 1909 when his horse Minoru won the Derby. Tens of thousands of people sang 'God Save the King' and cheered constantly. 'They indulged a delirious abandon which relieves very occasionally the reserve to which most Englishmen become habituated; and even the stolid policemen . . . threw care to the winds, waved helmets in the air, and joined jockeys, peers, shopkeepers and touts in yelling "Good old Teddy! Teddy boy! Hurrah! Hurrah!"'[23] The people may fairly be charged with volatility, yet it seems unlikely that those who cheered so loudly at Epsom had been among the foremost in condemning the Prince's penchant for baccarat. Kings are no different to the rest of humanity in being admired more by some than by others, and what to many of his people seemed raffish and dissolute vulgarity to another group was no more than robust manliness.

Edward VII was unusual, however, in the depth of disapproval and affection he encountered, and as he at last matured from what to many seemed an intolerably protracted adolescence so the grounds for disapproval dwindled. His conduct in private may have deserved little respect, but his public image became that of a dignified old buffer, self-indulgent, no doubt, but sedate, responsible and a natural father-figure. At his death the man in the street felt a personal sense of pain; as a widely-circulated broadsheet put it, it was:

> Greatest sorrow England ever had
> When death took away our dear Dad:
> A King was he from head to sole
> Loved by his people one and all.[24]

It takes time to become a father-figure. George V was to become far more the 'dear Dad' of his people than Edward

'I know, Sir, that you will maintain the prestige of the Title.
It would be impossible to increase it.'

VII had ever been, but he got away to a troubled start. When he slipped on mounting his horse he was accused of drunkenness; he was said to have left a morganatic wife and two children in Malta; Queen Mary was held to have married him too soon after the death of his brother and her former fiancé. That he overcame such suspicions was above all due to the profound and wholly sincere love which he bore his subjects. In 1905 he had visited India as Prince of Wales. His tour confirmed him in the belief, in Harold Nicolson's phrase, 'that there existed some almost mystical association between the Sovereign and the common people'.[25] That association he proceeded to cultivate with fervour, constantly visiting the great industrial centres and showing an interest in and enthusiasm for the proletariat which would have seemed grotesque to his predecessor. In 1912 King and Queen visited Cadeby colliery and went down a mine. Late that same night they heard there had been an accident in which seventy-eight miners were killed. The royal couple drove back at once to express their sympathy. It was hardly an extravagant gesture, yet few earlier kings would have done as much. On his last night in the West Riding he was serenaded by a miners' choir. He stepped out to greet them: 'My friends, it has been a great pleasure to us to visit your homes and see you at your daily work. We are deeply touched by the reception given to us wherever we have been . . . a reception which we shall never forget and which made us feel we were among true friends.'[26] None of those listening can have doubted that he meant what he said. 'He was a very wonderful King,' reminisced an old age pensioner many years later. 'He changed life completely from Edward VII's way.'[27]

The war cemented the relationship. The rapport which had developed between the King and the factory workers enabled him to make direct appeals for harder work in a way which could have been perilous for a politician. Even Lloyd George would have been hesitant before venturing into Tyneside and urging a massed audience of shipyard workers to abolish 'all restrictive rules and regulations'. 'There can be no question,' wrote Lloyd George in gratitude, 'that one outstanding reason for the high level of loyalty and patriotic effort which the people of this country maintained was the attitude and conduct of King George.'[28] He was equally assiduous in his visits to the army: 'He didn't stay in his country but went out with the troops,' a veteran remembered with nostalgia in 1960.[29] Yet not everyone found him such a paragon. In April 1917 H. G. Wells wrote to *The Times* to urge a republic and deplore the spectacle of Britain struggling on under 'an alien and uninspiring court'. 'I may be uninspiring,' grumbled the King, 'but I'll be damned if I'm alien.'[30] The rejoinder was characteristic of the bluff good sense that so appealed to his subjects.

On Christmas Day 1932 George V made a dramatic step forward in the field of public relations. He spoke to the nation on radio, an innovation that would anyway have seemed daring to his people and which his mastery of the medium speedily turned into a triumph. 'His was a wonderful voice,' wrote Harold Nicolson, 'strong, emphatic, vibrant, with undertones of sentiment, devoid of all condescension, artifice or prose.'[31] The King's Christmas-Day speech became a tradition almost before it had begun, a feature of the celebrations as significant and as immutable as holly, the Christmas tree or Midnight Mass.

His apotheosis came with the Silver Jubilee in 1935. Every day he drove out through streets packed to bursting point with his cheering subjects, every day he appeared on the balcony of Buckingham Palace to salute the rapturous crowds. Even the magistrates of Southport joined in the fun by allowing children under fourteen to see films usually open only to adults. 'I'd no idea they felt like that about me,' he remarked with tears in his eyes as he returned from one particularly triumphant tour of the East End. 'I'm beginning to think they must like me for myself.'[32] Not even the most cynical of observers could deny that there seemed to be some very real bond between monarch and people, a direct personal affection that was startling in its force. 'An immense spontaneous demonstration of good humour,' Kingsley Martin described the scene; a carnival equalled only by the armistice celebrations in 1918 yet unlike those almost wholly without drunkenness or hysteria.[33] On the night of 6 May the King once more addressed his people. 'At the close of this memorable day I must speak to my people everywhere. How can I express what is in my heart? I can only say to you, my very, very dear people, that the Queen and I thank you from the depths of our hearts for all the loyalty and – may I say so? – the love with which this day and always you have surrounded us. I dedicate myself anew to your service, for all the years that may still be given me ...' The words were, perhaps, neither startling nor sublime, yet the simplicity and the patent sincerity must have moved almost every listener.

'Crown and People' is a two-way affair. What the people really think of their king may be difficult to establish, what the King thinks of his people is almost impossible. Nevertheless there are moments when the defences slip and a flash of real feeling is to be detected. George V's speech to his people on Jubilee Day was one such moment; yet so, for that matter, was the expression of distaste, caught for posterity, on the face of the then Queen a few years later as she picked her way through a group of dejected and no doubt smelly citizens huddled in some public building the day after their homes had been destroyed in an air-raid. Was one reaction more truly representative of the monarch's feelings than the other? Almost certainly yes – the Queen's expression no more indicated contempt or dislike than the grimace of a mother mopping up her baby's vomit. Yet such instants of unwariness are valuable because they remind one that kings and queens too are people; capable of being repelled or outraged yet also able to exhibit real love for their subjects, something of a wholly different character from the platitudes that normally serve as a substitute for feeling. In

May 1935 George V's defences were down and his love for his people welled over in an exhibition of emotion which at other times he would have deplored.

The following year he died. Once again Kingsley Martin, hardly the most ardent of royalists, can be quoted in testimony of the popular dismay. 'No one who talked to his neighbour on a bus, to the charwoman washing the steps or to a sightseer standing at the street corner, could doubt the almost universal feeling of loss, nor could any perceptive observer fail to notice the peculiarly personal character of this emotion. People who had never seen the King and only heard his voice on the wireless talked about him as if he were a personal friend or a near relative.' Probably the funerals of Queen Victoria and of King George VI were the only others of the twentieth century which could compare with this for the intensity of regret shown by the public. The grief felt for someone personally known and loved must always be of a different quality to that felt for even the most admirable of strangers, yet George V seemed to have gone some way to closing that gap, to bringing the intimacy of private sorrow into the pomp of public mourning.

'People constantly reiterated that King George was "a father to us all"',' continued Kingsley Martin: 'he had become a universal father figure.' 'A fatherly person who loved his people', 'a real father to his nation', were but two of the many similar recollections of him by his subjects twenty years later. 'Father-figure', one of those phrases that trips in loving incomprehension off the tongue of every amateur psychiatrist, is best used with circumspection. When the paternal image is invoked by quite so many people, however, it cannot be ignored. George V was identified in the popular mind with benevolent authority. Only the most naïve can have believed that he possessed the power actually to reshape their lives; yet his influence over the politicians and the executive was held – not without some reason – to be considerable. He stood for absolute standards of decency and stability in a world of self-questioning and shifting values; with his death the average citizen felt that much less secure about the future. The death of a father causes alarm as well as grief: the mourning for King George V was mixed with a vague disquiet.

In *A Favourite of the Gods* Sybille Bedford's heroine Constanza is reprimanded by her mother for a lack of respect towards the royal family. 'Well, you know, mama, I'm rather anti-monarchy. Yes, yes, I know it's extremely *mal vu* here, a republican is worse than a socialist – I can't help it. Constitutional monarchies have their uses, but why keep the trappings? Like primitive and organized religion, and it's all so bourgeois.' To be both primitive and organized, to appeal to the latent romantic in every bourgeois without disturbing his prosaic preoccupations, was the achievement of twentieth-century monarchy, brought to a fine art by George V. 'You haven't seen their pearls,' was the lapidary retort of Constanza's mother. Constanza would have found a readier response from King Edward VIII. Edward deplored both the trappings and the bourgeois values of the monarchy. He believed that the royal family must be progressive and relevant; whether in terms of cocktails, jazzy and raffish friends or of an alliance with the more radical elements of society in an assault upon the staid and timorous establishment.

The lines of battle were set in a celebrated conversation between Edward, then Prince of Wales, and Sir Frederick Ponsonby. Ponsonby argued: 'The monarchy must always retain an element of mystery. A Prince should not show himself too much. The monarchy must remain on a pedestal.' The Prince of Wales said that, on the contrary, it should be brought down to the people. Ponsonby retorted that, if it lost its mystery, loss of its influence would quickly follow.[34] At first the Prince's campaign to bring the monarchy to the people worked well. With the expenditure of remarkably little effort or serious thought he contrived to pass himself off as the champion of the workers, the socially conscious radical who revolted against the greed and inhumanity of capitalist society. 'Something must be done,' the King's shocked response to the horrors of unemployment in South Wales, typified admirably the genuine good-will as well as the superficiality of his approach. As late as 1964 he was remembered with affection and, for 3% of those asked, was still their favourite member of the royal family. Remarks by working-class admirers – 'If he'd stayed on the throne the working people would have been better off'; 'He was closer to the people than any of them and we would have seen great changes'; 'He did a lot for the miners and used to go out and see things for himself' – show how his sedulously fostered image had lingered on.[35]

Whether it would have long survived the harsh trials of life upon the throne is another matter. To drink to the king over the water is one thing, actually to serve under him when the bonny boat has sped him back again calls for different qualities on the part of both monarch and subject. When the crisis caused by the King's determination to marry Mrs Simpson burst on a dismayed public the initial reaction of many was that he should be allowed to marry whom he liked. 'He broke the rules of the marriage of royalty and showed he was a *man*,' was the epitaph bestowed on him by one motor mechanic, who never saw cause to change his views. In the first days after the news broke 90% of the letters received by the national newspapers were said to be in favour of the King.[36] Yet such support was quickly swept away in an avalanche of revulsion.

Two letters typify the root causes of this hostility. The first was written to the *Daily Express*. 'Isn't it very dreadful,' it asked, 'that Edward VIII, son of our Beloved King George, should bring Hollywood ideals to Britain? Surely he could have found some sweet British Girl?' Much the same point of view, if recorded in more sophisticated language, was expressed by Harold Nicolson in his diary. '. . . he imagines that the country, the great warm heart of the people, are with him. I do not think so. The upper classes mind her being an American more than they mind her being divorced. The lower classes do not mind her being an American but loathe the idea that she has two husbands already.'[37] The King had been guilty of vulgarity; he had betrayed the standards which, in the eyes of most of his people, it was his duty to protect. The King must personify those virtues of decency and family loyalty which had been so apparent in the conduct of his father. If he could not do so then he was not fit to rule.

The second letter, written to though not published in the *Morning Post*, exemplifies a still more fundamental sense of outrage. 'How can the Defender of the Faith,' it asked, 'betray the most sacred principles of the Church and still retain his position? Solemnly to crown him as the Elect of God would be to desecrate Westminster Abbey and to turn this noble ceremony into a blasphemous farce!' At any time it is unwise to underestimate the force of religious feeling among the British people; even in 1956 34% of those questioned still believed that the Queen was someone specially chosen by God and in 1964 the figure had only dropped to 30%.[38] Any speculation about the results of a similar poll in 1937 must be rash; yet, given the far more overt role played by religion in the lives of the average Briton, it would be surprising if less than half the population would then have seen some special link between God and King. In January 1937, when names were being suggested for the infant Princess Alexandra, a reader wrote to the *Observer* to comment that, among the many proposals, none 'sufficiently marks the extraordinary miracle of a royal birth in a time of great national stress'. No one who believed that the birth of a junior princess, remote from the direct line of succession, could smack even distantly of the miraculous would be able to view with equanimity the elevation of a woman with three living husbands to the throne of Britain.

Many people, among them some of the most articulate and persuasive in the realm, argued the contrary, but to most of those whose task it was to interpret the feelings of the public it seemed that opposition was almost visibly hardening day by day. 'And now 'ere we 'ave this obstinate little man with 'is Mrs Simpson,' said J. H. Thomas to Harold Nicolson. 'Hit won't do, 'arold, I tell you that straight. I know the people of this country. I *know* them. They 'ate 'aving no family life at Court.'[39] At a meeting in a church hall in Islington only ten out of 400 people rose for the national anthem. 'I never dreamed,' said the Rev. Mr Paxton sadly, 'that I should live to see the day when my congregation refused to sing "God Save the King".'[40] A fox-hunting squire from Wales, himself in the throes of a somewhat messy divorce, pronounced that, 'The King was no gentleman'. The words might have been different but the sense was echoed at every level of society. 'It wouldn't have done,' a taxi-driver concluded. 'It wouldn't have done.'

Once the die was cast the British people found plenty of reasons to justify a decision that had been mainly intuitive and emotional. A microcosm of public opinion, recollected in tranquillity, was exhibited in the waiting-room of a railway station shortly after the death of King George VI, where long delay overcame the reluctance of the British traveller to admit the existence of his fellow sufferers. A Mass Observer happened to be present:

Man, 60ish, middle-class:	'Things would have been very different if the other chap – the Fascist – had come to the throne.'
Observer:	'Do you think he was a Fascist? I never heard that.'
Woman, 55ish, lower middle-class:	'Oh yes. He was all linked up with *them*, you know, the Cliveden Set. They were forming a King's party.'
Man, 60ish:	'There'd have been civil war if that chap had become King.

	This country would have been a republic by now.'
Man, 55ish, lower middle-class:	'I've nothing against the Duke of Windsor. I met him in the trenches in the First World War. He was a toff.'
Man, 60ish:	'He was a waster. No force of character. If he'd been King...'

The arrival of the train cut short what was about to become a heated discussion.[41]

The problem of how far the popular rejection of Edward VIII and Mrs Simpson was the fruit of a campaign led by the press and how far it would have existed anyway, merely finding a voice in the newspapers, is in a sense the theme of this book. Prior to 1937 techniques for establishing the thoughts and feelings of the people hardly existed. Mass Observation pioneered both an awareness of the need for an enquiry and a means of conducting it. Since then the machinery for the accumulation of statistical data about the national mood has grown more sophisticated. Yet even now only the most optimistic would claim that they could unerringly analyse national opinion on any given issue, still less explain why it had formed or why, perhaps in the space of a few days or even hours, it might well change fundamentally. One can only state as a matter of opinion, not susceptible of proof, that it seems the great majority of the British people was repelled by the concept of Mrs Simpson on the throne. That this primitive reaction was improperly used by the politicians to force matters to the point of abdication is a line which can be argued, but even those who do so would scarcely deny that the reaction existed, and was almost entirely spontaneous. It sprang from an exalted vision of the monarchy and of the standards which it represented, a vision that had been tarnished often enough in the past but never so totally demolished. If George

V, above all, had not conducted himself so signally as a king, his son's dereliction from duty might not have seemed so unforgivable to his people.

'Sir,' said Baldwin to the new King, 'if I may say so, you need have no fear for the future. The whole country is behind you with a deep and understanding sympathy.'[42] He exaggerated. The abdication gave a fillip to those people who favoured the abolition of the monarchy. In the House of Commons Jimmy Maxton pleaded that the opportunity should be taken of sweeping away the whole anachronistic tradition and opening the way for a truly democratic form of government. His amendment was defeated by 403 votes to five, but the Tory MP Sir Arnold Wilson guessed that in a free vote on this issue as many as 100 members might have voted for a republic.[43] *The Times* claimed that the abdication strengthened the principle of constitutional monarchy by making clear that it was to be viewed 'not in terms of personal affection for an individual but in the prosaic terms of a working institution'. In the long term this was probably proved true, but in 1936 the monarchy had suffered a blow which even some of its supporters felt it might not survive.

Certainly George VI mounted the throne in an atmosphere of muted enthusiasm. When he drove out to take his first levee at St James's only a handful of spectators watched his progress. 'Not many of them, are there, my lady?' said a maid to a lady-in-waiting with gloomy relish.[44] There was similar coolness when the royal family left for Sandringham for Christmas in 1936. The representative of the *New York Herald Tribune* was among those present and noticed how few others had taken the trouble to come, in spite of the attention paid to the event in the newspapers.

King George VI, hat in hand, bowed right and left automatically as he drove up. Scarcely a hat was raised in reply . . . King George VI and his family walked

39

The Choice

The Prime Minister: 'All the peoples of your Empire, Sir, sympathize with you most deeply; but they all know – as you yourself must – that the throne is greater than the man.'

bowing across the platform. Perhaps half the men in the little throng raised their hats. There was a subdued murmur which might have been a suppressed cheer – or might not. In short, on his first public appearance after his succession to his brother, King George VI was given an extremely cold shoulder.[45]

The correspondent for this particular newspaper was unlikely to be prejudiced in favour of the monarchy, but even *The Times* gave an impression of a small crowd and a far from rapturous reception.

Nevertheless the new King had some useful cards in his hand. As Duke of York he had established a reputation for conscientious if unspectacular hard work, had made a speciality of industrial relations and had spent much time trudging around those dingier areas of the United Kingdom which his brother would have found insufficiently glamorous to merit his attention. His youth camps, at which every year 200 public schoolboys and 200 youths from factories spent a week together in games and other communal activities, had proved a triumphant success. By nature shy and unobtrusive, he had never tried to emerge from the shadow of his more flamboyant brother, but within that shadow he had become known as a *good* man, a man of integrity and decency, above all a safe man who could be relied on not to kick over the traces or in any way outrage public opinion. 'There goes the hope of England,' a man had cried as the Duke of York left Buckingham Palace at the time of the Jubilee. Not many people would then have joined in the cry, but now it was widely felt that he was indeed a hope for the future. If he had been a man in the mould of his brother then the voice of republicanism would have been heard loudly in the land; as it was, the existence of an acceptable substitute ensured that the institution was in little danger.

The two young Princesses were his greatest asset, more than redeeming in the public favour the Duke of York's inability to assert himself as an extrovert or brilliant figure. There was little reason to expect that either Princess Elizabeth or Margaret Rose would succeed to the throne, but with Edward VIII unmarried the public had transferred to them the almost obsessive interest which it takes in the inhabitants of royal nurseries. Their most trivial deed was lovingly chronicled; the decision to clothe them in yellow rather than in blue could change the fashion for a generation. When 'Lillibet' did not accompany her father on a visit to Edinburgh the Duke wrote to tell his mother how much she had been missed. 'It almost frightens me that the people should love her so much. I suppose that it is a good thing, and I hope that she will be worthy of it, poor little darling.'[46]

The family was to be the key-note of the new reign – that and a return to the other bourgeois virtues which had been paramount under King George V. According to Dermot Morrah, one of the most reliable of royal chroniclers, the new Queen 'insisted that the unbending must be left to her, and that the crowned and anointed King must not be too ready to step down from his pedestal'.[47] Even if the Queen had not so insisted the King would have reached a similar conclusion. By conviction, by temperament and from an awareness of his own limitations, he was determined to play a more aloof and retiring role than would have suited his elder brother. After their brief brush with another style of monarchy, this unexciting prospect appeared entirely acceptable to the British people.

CHAPTER TWO

Coronation, 1937

The Coronation of a British monarch is the event which brings him more dramatically than any other to the forefront of his people's consciousness. Only his death can earn comparable attention, and on that occasion there can hardly be the obsessive build-up by newspapers and other communications media which marks the former happening. Everything in the preceding months is designed to place the monarch at the centre of the stage and reduce even the most imposing of the other participants – be they Archbishop, Prime Minister or foreign grandee – into members of a supporting cast. It is a time at which even those least inclined to think about the royal family or the nature of monarchy can hardly avoid committing themselves to some opinion. It is a moment of revelation: when generally inarticulate loyalty is loudly voiced; latent hostility exposed; the cautious attitudes of every day transformed into avid interest or sated distaste.

Yet the precise significance of this antique ceremony is hard to establish in constitutional, religious or any other terms. '*Le roi est mort, vive le roi.*' George VI had been king since his brother's abdication, and whatever powers he enjoyed were in no whit augmented by the rituals acted out on 12 May 1937. William IV tried to do without the ceremony altogether; if the war had come shortly after the accession it seems highly unlikely that George VI would have been crowned until peace returned. 'If the successor is to become King in the fullest sense,' wrote Professor Schramm in his

43

History of the English Coronation, 'he must first be inaugurated
into the government by legal and ecclesiastical rites.'[1]
The words 'fullest sense' raise more questions than they
answer. Since in practical terms the royal power is already
complete the significance of the Coronation must presumably be mystical. Through the medium of the Church of
England divine sanction is being invoked for the monarch,
an element of the sacred is investing an institution which
otherwise is judged primarily in political, economic or
social terms. 'I had a sudden feeling,' wrote Margaret Lane
of a later Coronation in the somewhat unexpected pages of
the *New Statesman,*[2] '. . . a sensation that was like something
spoken aloud: "There is a secret here." . . . What that
secret was, I could not say. No doubt it was the primitive
and magical feeling which ancient and beautiful ceremonials
still invoke, no matter in how rational a breast.' Certainly
anyone who tried to analyse the impact of King George
VI's Coronation on the British people without taking some
account of latent beliefs and impulses far removed from the
tidy categories of the professional sociologist would end up
with a misleading picture.

But to maintain that the Coronation instilled a disquiet,
a real if no doubt transitory reverence into normally
phlegmatic and materialistic minds, while probably true,
does not get one very far. Is it possible to be more precise
about the effects of the ceremony on those who, one way or
another, participated in or observed it? Were the behaviour
patterns of the British people in any way affected by the
events of 12 May? The particular importance of the Coronation is that it is the moment at which Church and State
unite in exaltation of a form of government. 'The Constitu-
tion is made legitimate by being brought into contact with
the sacred,' observed Dr Bocock,[3] and it is at the Coronation
more than on any other occasion that the monarch explicitly
espouses the Christian ethic and accepts it as the basis for
his government. The fact that the monarch no longer
effectively governs, little diminishes the ritual significance

of such an affirmation.

A coronation, therefore, provides both a defence of the established order and a promise that it will conduct itself in the future according to civilized and 'Christian' values. Its effect on the minds of the people, if it has any, will be predominantly conservative. Whether or not this should be considered a good thing depends upon one's attitude towards the existing state of society. The point is well illustrated by a controversy that was conducted in 1955 in the pages of the *Sociological Review* between Professor Shils and Dr Michael Young on the one hand and Professor Birnbaum on the other.[4] The debate was remarkable not so much for the quality of the evidence or the objectivity of the argument as for the admirably robust if unscientific way in which both parties propounded value-judgements and aired their prejudices on a startlingly small basis of established data. To Shils and Young the Coronation was a 'rededication' and 'an act of national communion', affirming the moral values by which society lived – 'generosity, charity, loyalty, justice in the distribution of opportunities and rewards, reasonable respect for authority, the dignity of the individual and his right to freedom'; establishing the existence of a 'general moral consensus of society'. To Birnbaum these 'tinsel revels' were no more than a prop to an unfair social order, a self-interested effort on the part of the rulers to blind the ruled to the iniquitous nature of the system which encompassed them. Both views have the merit of simplicity and both accept that the overall effect of a coronation is likely to be the readier acceptance by the Briton of the society in which he lives.

What Shils and Young described as 'reasonable respect for authority' is no less apparent in the familial aspect of the Coronation. The symbolism of King George VI as the father of his people was reinforced by the emphasis placed by the publicity media on the King as *père de famille*. The King as a happily married man and father of two attractive daughters was exalted in contrast to his brother, childless and now married to a divorcée. The picture of a devoted and smiling family was projected in innumerable variants and presented, both explicitly and implicitly, as the symbol of a national or, still wider, imperial family. Unlike a football match or many of the other jamborees with which the Coronation is sometimes equated the normal unit of participation was the family: parents and children clustered round the radio; if you decided to take a look at what was going on in all probability you took the kids along with you. It would be a bold man who spoke too categorically of cause and effect, yet it is not without interest that substantially fewer actions for divorce were started in the twelve months after the Coronation than in the twelve months before it.

If the man in the street had been asked what the Coronation meant to him it is doubtful if he would have replied in terms of social order or family ties. If there were reactions in such fields they were largely subliminal, absorbed into the subconscious rather than overtly imbibed. To many people the Coronation was little more than a welcome holiday, an excuse for a party or an extra drink, a break from the routine. Yet even among the most cynical or uninterested there was often felt an unexpected thrill of national pride. 'The Coronation,' wrote the anthropologist, Professor Malinowski, 'was, among other things, a large-scale ceremonial display of the greatness, power and wealth of Britain . . . Even if the ceremony be taken at its lowest as a large piece of window dressing, it might still have been well-invested expenditure. Psychologically, I think, there was no doubt that the Coronation generated an increased feeling of security, of stability, and the permanence of the British Empire.'[5] Patriotism, sometimes almost unwillingly expressed, is one reaction commonly encountered among those whose testimonies comprise the Mass Observation Archive for the 1937 Coronation.

A sense of national unity was also frequently experienced. However spurious Professor Birnbaum would have deemed it, a feeling of community does seem to have gripped Great

Britain in the weeks before the ceremony and still more on
12 May. Though attitudes differed, virtually everybody was
preoccupied by the same event. This common focus of
attention broke down the traditional inhibitions, so that the
subject might be as freely discussed between strangers,
and emotions as freely shared, as at the time of the final of
the World Cup between England and West Germany in
1966. Class barriers seemed less significant. 'The important
thing to remember,' one of the grandest of British grandees
remarked, 'is that in the eyes of the royal family we're all
glorified footmen and ladies' maids.' There is some exaggera-
tion in the comment, but it expresses an important truth:
that duke and peasant are both subjects, equal not only
before God but, to some extent at least, before their monarch.

But national unity was not incompatible with a highly
developed sense of community. Fierce local loyalty flourished,
particularly in the suburbs of the great cities and the smaller
villages. Each street party, each bonfire on the village green,
seemed intended not merely to honour the crowning of the
King but to show the benighted inhabitants of the vicinity
that its organizers could put on a better show than anybody
else. Trespassers from outside were treated with suspicion
if not actually expelled. Sometimes, indeed, the emphasis
was placed so heavily on local achievement that the casual
observer would hardly have known that there was a Coronation at all.

Typical remarks heard in South Norwood on the eve
of the ceremony were: 'How impressed foreigners must be!';
'And so good for trade, my dear'; 'The man I feel most
sorry for is the King'. All coronations follow broadly the
same pattern but all have their individual *leitmotif,* and the
Coronation of 1937 was tinged by a sense of pity for the
King who had been flung so brutally into a role for which
he was not prepared and which he was known to dread.
No one was more conscious than George VI that the monarchy had been shaken by the abdication crisis, that some
at least of those who watched felt Edward VIII would have

filled the throne far better, that others felt there was little point in a royal family whose members conducted themselves no better, perhaps even worse than was the custom among their subjects. The theme of his daughter's Coronation was to be regeneration; the birth of a new Britain under a new Elizabeth. For George VI there could be nothing so ambitious. 'Consolidation' was the theme; the restatement of traditional values; the affirmation that, in spite of all that had happened, business was as usual, the monarchy carried on.

Consolidation lacks drama. It is human nature to remember the past in rosy terms: no summers are so hot, no cricketers so splendid as those enjoyed in youth. Yet of 139 people who, from personal experience, compared the Coronations of 1937 and 1953 sixty-eight considered the latter to be the more memorable and only four opted for the former.[6] A further twenty-four declared that – usually to their surprise – they could recall nothing of the earlier event, the implication being that they would have done so if it had matched in grandeur or attraction the Coronation of Queen Elizabeth. The earlier Coronation was 'a very tame affair compared with this'; there was 'much less excitement and interest beforehand'; everything in 1953 was 'better organized or rehearsed'. Not everyone put it in such flattering terms. There was 'less fuss and nonsense' in 1937 was an opinion expressed by several, but the net result was still that they had found the impact weaker. Even of those four who championed the 1937 Coronation the reason given by one of them, that it was 'a great deal less vulgar and, for this reason, far more impressive', suggests that she was conscious of the superior force of the contemporary version. Several reasons were given for the difference: the 'young and beautiful Queen'; the relative lack of glamour of her father, 'unknown', 'retiring', 'sincere but not romantic'; the shadow cast by the abdication; above all the impact of television. Whatever the causes, however, almost 95% stated – implicitly or explicitly – that the Coronation of 1937 was altogether less extravagant and assertive.

Not that extravagance and assertiveness were rare in the months preceding the Coronation. The British public was bombarded with information about every aspect of the coming festivity. There was a curious obsession with the physical details of the arrangements. The Office of Works, reported the *News Chronicle*, was to provide seating for 90,000; 3 million feet of tubing would be needed and 850 tons of Columbian pine. The Coronation Procession, revealed the *Daily Mail*, would be 3500 yards long and would take forty minutes to pass any given point. The total weight of the equipment the BBC would use within Westminster Abbey, the *Daily Dispatch* told its readers, was twelve tons and they would be using approximately 472 miles of wire. Any statistic was welcome provided it testified to the grandeur and lavishness of the occasion. Two hundred thousand visitors from overseas were expected including the Count of Flanders, the Crown Prince of Denmark, Prince Chichibu from Japan, Mr Litvinoff from Russia and Miss Sheila Martin of Wagga Wagga, selected as the 'best representative of Australian girlhood'. The media displayed their traditional fascination with their own activities; the coverage to be afforded by the BBC was studied with particular care since for the first time microphones were to be installed all over the Abbey, and it was thought that listeners might even hear the King's voice during part of the service. The *Daily Mirror* was gratified to report that the Archbishop of Canterbury, 'ever vigilant of public interest and good taste', would scan the news films of the Coronation as soon as they were available and cut from the record 'anything which may be considered unsuitable for the public at large to see'.

Nor was the provincial press backward in reporting the plans of their localities. The *Midland Daily Telegraph* announced that in Coventry no less than five special committees of the City Council had drawn up a programme which would include football and baseball matches, ox-roasting, open-air dancing, a firework display, a sports meeting and a Coronation Ball. At Croydon, claimed the *Croydon Times*, 3000 old age pensioners would be invited to tea and an entertainment; the blind would get supper and an entertainment in the large public hall while the deaf and dumb would receive a cup of tea and refreshments. In Hastings, according to the *Sunday Referee*, the Coronation sports meeting would include an event in which couples (a man and a girl) wearing ordinary clothes over bathing costumes, would have to undress and then put on each other's clothes.

Except for those directly involved with the arrangements, however, it does not seem that interest in the Coronation was generally great until a few weeks before the event. Three Mass Observers – a non-political male of twenty-eight working in a cotton mill; a nineteen-year-old male bank clerk of mildly left-wing views and a non-political twenty-six-year-old housewife from near Birmingham – kept full records of what they said and did on 12 March, two months before the event. Only one of them even mentioned the Coronation and then only to record that a colleague showed him an advertisement for a periscope while another tried to sell him a Coronation tie.[7]

Commercial interests were indeed active in whipping up interest in the celebrations. Endless ingenuity was displayed in twisting various facets of the festivities into a form where they could promote a product. '*N'kosi, N'kosi, Bayete,*' proclaimed an advertisement in the *Radio Times*. 'This is the royal salute of the Zulus ... With a single voice on Coronation Day the myriad tongues of Africa will unite in thunderous homage to the King-Emperor. Then warriors will be at one with workers – the men, for instance, whose toil in the plantations of Rhodesia and Nyasaland helps to bring your Three Nuns Empire Blend to its perfection.' Selfridges employed eighteen sculptors for twelve months on their decorations, a series of panels representing episodes in British history from the time of the Druids to Armistice Day. Drages welcomed the Coronation with 'Music, Pageantry, Colour and Souvenir Gifts to all customers'. A butcher pressed galantines of pork into coronet shapes and cased them in crimson jelly. 'Have you the energy to attend to-morrow's rehearsal?' asked the manufacturers of Eno's Fruit Salts. 'Or do you feel drowsy and heavy, and find it's a hard job to get out of bed?' 'Cash in on the Coronation!' advised a trade journal brashly. 'Give your shop a patriotic effect.'

Sometimes things were taken too far and led to protests. 'As an Englishman,' wrote an indignant patriot on 28 April, 'I was disgusted to see displayed in the shop window . . . a Union Jack in the form of a rug and I would like to appeal to those who have fought for our flag in the past . . . to remonstrate against this desecration of our national emblem.' But such outbursts were rare: in general the excesses of commerce passed unnoticed or were accepted as part of the inevitable vulgarization of public life. 'I think it benefits the country to have a Coronation,' said a chef of thirty-one, 'in that it puts money into circulation pretty quickly: example, the men who were selling periscopes did a roaring trade, then there is the sale of the national colours, then again on the social side in the higher circles, and the catering, and travelling agents.' It is noteworthy that none of those who praised the Coronation as a stimulus to trade went on to argue that it also led to an influx of tourists from abroad and valuable foreign currency.

Business men were not the only people to pursue their private interests under a cloak of royalism. The Coronation season, suggested one enthusiast, should be 'a fitting time for a special effort to gladden the hearts of British dogs'. Was this not the occasion, asked another, for a compact to refrain from picking wild flowers in any place to which the public had access? Pet schemes were resurrected: the revival of maypole dancing in one place, the elevation of

Portsmouth to the status of a royal borough in another. There was no shortage of busybodies ready and anxious to stir the pot of public interest.

By April no further stirring was needed; though the level of enthusiasm might vary it was becoming more and more difficult to avoid *some* reaction to the proliferation of publicity for the Coronation. A peculiar feature, presumably inspired by the unhappy circumstances in which George VI had come to the throne, was the number of reports that, for one reason or another, the ceremony would never take place. 'There won't be no Coronation,' pronounced a newspaper man at Lewisham. 'The King will be dead by then. He's dying on his feet. They're keeping him alive artificially.' A charwoman at Blackheath was equally confident, though her reason, reluctantly vouchsafed when pressed, was that 'everybody wanted the Duke of Windsor back'. Bradford business men were said to be betting against a Coronation taking place. The proprietress of a stationer's shop was asked if she had heard the rumours and replied: 'Oh yes, a good many people are saying so. I'm sure I don't know why. I expect they must be Communists.' Everyone seemed to have a friend who had a friend who had met a gipsy prophesying doom – in the Monument Road of Birmingham, between Dymchurch and New Romney, in Ashford, near Brighton. 'They didn't ought to say such a thing after all the money that's been spent,' commented a Birmingham charwoman.

Criticism of the new King and of the ceremony itself was scarce, insignificant indeed if one looks back to the early nineteenth century and considers the furore that greeted George IV's intemperate extravagance. Usually it consisted of more or less routine denunciations of the great expense, money which would have been better spent on a multitude of worthy projects. 'We are going to burn £200 in a fire on Leith Links,' wrote an indignant ratepayer to the *Edinburgh Evening News*. 'Do we expect the disabled and unemployed ex-Service men . . . to gather round with their wives and children and throw up their caps in jubilation . . .?' There were also the protests of those who saw not only that money would be wasted on frivolity but that they themselves would personally be out of pocket as a result Lancashire weavers and coalminers from Treharris were among those who protested at losing some or all of a day's pay while a number of leading musicians were reported to be unwilling to play in the special orchestra in Westminster Abbey on account of the low pay offered.

A form of criticism was to opt out, to proclaim that the Coronation was no affair of yours and that you proposed to pursue your own devices. 'Do you know what I'm going to do on Coronation Day?' asked an elderly lady who owned a small café in Birmingham. 'Me and the girls are going to cut the bottoms off the blinds at home, where they've got dirty, and then sew them up again.' A Mass Observer whose husband's hobby was bee-keeping said that he was thoroughly bored with the whole business and proposed to spend the day opening his hives. A greengrocer was going to be busy in his greenhouse. An extreme example came from Norfolk where a baby was due on Coronation Day. 'They did it on purpose,' said the midwife indignantly. 'They counted up and found that they had to commit the act on their little girl's birthday.' In this last case there could be no turning back, but it is noteworthy that, where the movements of the self-proclaimed opter-out can be followed on 12 May, symptoms of guilt or curiosity were often experienced early in the morning and their victim was likely to spend the day as firmly attached to the radio as any of his more royalist neighbours.

One of the problems of risking even tentative generalizations on the basis of what people have been heard to say is, of course, that the mere act of saying something indicates a degree of concern. Apathy is usually dumb. There may well have been a large but hidden minority who cared little about the Coronation but were not disposed to criticize it overtly. Of those who ventured an opinion, however, there can be no doubt that the vast majority – 90% probably of the several hundred whose views are featured one way or another in the Mass Observation Archive – were looking forward to the day with some eagerness and planning how best to enjoy an occasion which seemed unlikely to recur for many years. The sort of problems which perplexed them – petty, even ridiculous, yet important to those concerned – are well exemplified in the meeting of the Coronation Committee of a certain local authority at 7.30 p.m. on 26 April 1937.

The purpose of the meeting was primarily to decide the composition of the special souvenir programme. After a foreword by the Chairman of the Council there were to follow short biographies of the King, the Queen and other members of the royal family. The town clerk felt that these were inaccurate; the chairman thought that 'the less said about the royal family's private life the better'. The item was deleted. After the text of the proclamation and some photographs there followed a genealogical table. The town clerk thought this was inaccurate too. Councillor X thought it 'interesting to trace back the descent of the King; he could himself trace his ancestors back to 1730 . . .' Councillor Y did not agree. The item was deleted. First event on the programme was a march to church by the Girl Guides. Councillor Z thought 'the Guides were going to church by train . . . and in any case nobody was very interested in them.' The item was deleted. Next came a 'patriotic play' given by the local dramatic society. Councillor Z pointed out that this had nothing to do with the Council's activities, and that the proceeds were being given to a charity of which he did not approve. In view of the increasing slimness of the programme it was perhaps fortunate that the councillor was overruled and the item was not deleted. The liveliest exchange took place when Councillor Y discovered that there was to be a running buffet at the Coronation Ball.

'Mr Chairman: am I correct in understanding that intoxicating liquor is to be on sale at the ball?'

'That is so.'

'Then I must disassociate myself from it completely. I have never been so shocked in all my life, to think that we, as a Council, are sponsoring a ball at which intoxicating liquor will be sold. I am greatly upset; there is too much of that sort of thing in the public halls today. I have seen young girls reeling about under the influence of drink at dances when there has been no buffet; where, I believe, drink is brought in from outside.'

'That shows that it will make little difference. People will drink whether there is a buffet or not.'

'It will be much worse if drink is easily obtainable at a bar . . .'

Councillor Y proved to be alone in his objections, and this item too was not deleted. A brisk discussion then took place as to whether the bowling club should be given three trophies to present at a Coronation Tournament. It was decided that this would create an awkward precedent, in spite of a strong plea for magnanimity from Councillor R who argued that 'there would not be a Coronation every year, at least he hoped not'. It being ten past nine, the councillors then made a rush for their hats and coats while the town clerk disposed of the remaining business in a rapidly emptying chamber. Meanwhile at a typical meeting in a Norfolk village it was quickly decided to follow the precedents of the Jubilee. This involved sports and a tea of meat and beer. 'If you will pardon the vulgarity,' commented the postmaster, 'all they want is a gluttonous feast.'

By shortly before Coronation Day London was in ferment. Half a million people spent the best part of a night in the rain to see the final rehearsal of the Coronation procession from Buckingham Palace to Westminster at dawn on Sunday 9 May. Some 50,000 besieged the Palace the same night and cheered vociferously as the various members of the royal family began to foregather. By now there were 300,000 foreign visitors in London and vast crowds passed the days wandering up and down the route admiring the decorations. The only discordant notes were struck by the busmen who were on strike for extra wages. West End hotel waiters, taxi drivers and tramway workers were threatening to join in. There seems to have been no strong feeling about the strikers on the part of the general public, either of solidarity or of indignation, though some of the more elderly thought it a shame that the King should have his great day spoilt by such sectarian selfishness.

On the night of 11 May the centre of London hardly slept. An Observer passed Marble Arch at about 3.30 a.m. People were thronging towards the route from the Edgware Road:

> carrying parcels, boxes, rugs, children, flags, rucksacks etc. Lots of shocked comment on discovering that they are not first on the scene. I walk very quickly through Hyde Park section of route – identical scenes as Oxford Street – and here, in addition, the crowds are camping on the grass verge as well as the footway, so a few may sleep in a little comfort. By now a pathetic and sordid spectacle: everyone's weariness is apparent, couples mutter in each other's ears, close-folded in one another's arms under rugs and coats, children weep or mutter sleepily, young girls of twelve or so run about to keep warm and shout irritably to one another.

Slowly things got better. Cramped limbs were stretched, hot drinks gulped, warmth returned. People began to take an interest in what was happening around them. Anything was better than nothing. A policeman on a horse got a rousing cheer, scavengers collecting the dung dropped by the horses were greeted with laughter and enthusiasm. (The *Daily Express* had a 'cheermeter' to measure the reaction of the crowds. This instrument recorded that Queen Mary got the noisiest reception, then the King and Queen, then the dung-collectors.) In spite of the strains of the night it was an immensely tolerant and good-natured crowd. The police were assumed to be on the side of the audience and were greeted as friends, to be offered coffee or a bun and consulted about the problems of public lavatories. They, for their part, turned a blind eye to everything except the worst excesses. There was remarkably little resentment shown by those who had camped out along the route against the privileged seat-holders who arrived after a good night's sleep to watch the show in comfort. In Suffolk Street at about 5 a.m. 'waiters in evening dress in the empty lighted rooms of a club are arranging things on tables'; in Charles Street, 'seat-holders – silk hat and opera glasses, grey topper and grey waistcoat and button-hole – move slowly along. The smell of a Turkish cigarette'; yet they met at the worst with amiable mockery and rarely even that. Near Hyde Park Corner a car containing a grandly dressed dowager was met with a tap on the window and a cry of 'Oo! Carnival Queen!'

As the distant sound of bands heralded the approach of the procession there was a feverish rustle, a jostling for position which, while almost invariably polite and good-natured, still contained a tinge of desperation as people realized that the scene they had suffered so much discomfort to witness might after all escape them. Yet people were remarkably unselfish. Some men on the stands called to a woman on the pavement below to pass up her little children so that they could get a decent view. 'Will you please send them back as soon as the King and Queen have passed?' 'Yes, and the guns.' 'No, I don't want them to see the guns, only the King and Queen.' Tension grew, and one seems to detect a sense that people were *determined* to be excited, to enjoy themselves; that this was an *occasion* and they would be letting down themselves and the other participants if they failed to respond to it.

An introspective thirty-nine-year-old female typist of republican leanings analysed her feelings at the moment the procession reached her position:

I was surprised how much I responded to the atmosphere of the crowd, the cheering etc. I felt a definite pride and thrill in belonging to the Empire, which in ordinary life, with my political bias, is just the opposite of my true feelings. Yet I felt a definite sense of relief that I could experience this emotion and be in and of the crowd. One becomes very weary of always being in the minority, thinking things silly which other people care about; one must always be arguing, or repressing oneself, and it is psychologically very bad ... Therefore you will understand that the carnival spirit of the actual Coronation Day *really* was a holiday for me, and I say this without cynicism.

Recollecting her emotions in tranquillity this typist concluded that the capacity to create this sort of euphoria was too dangerous a weapon to be entrusted to those in authority and that she was confirmed in her republican views. She must have been – as she so clearly sensed – a lonely figure among the crowds. Though some were doubtless there from curiosity and others on the principle of 'know thy enemies' it is reasonable to assume that the London crowds contained a far higher proportion of ardent imperialists and royalists than would have been the case at a cup final or race meeting. It is not surprising therefore that a somewhat strident patriotism made itself heard. Britain was proving itself to the world. 'They've all got their answer today,' said a poorly dressed man to a neighbour who looked like a commercial traveller. 'We've called their bluff,' replied the other with an air of finality. A schoolmaster was stirred by the contingents from the Empire: 'It affected me to think that England's* influence reached so far.' Most people were sensitive to any suggestion that they were deficient in patriotism. A working-class man looking at a royal photograph remarked: 'Look at the old

* In London at least Britain seemed hardly to exist as a concept. It was England's day.

girl; she looks as if she's got toothache.' 'You're not very loyal, are you?' said a Mass Observer provocatively. 'Oh, I'm patriotic all right. I've been up all night waiting to see the procession.' 'Why did you do it?' 'Oh, something inside me made me, and after all it's nice to be able to tell your pals that you've seen it.'

It was inevitable that the royal couple should get the loudest cheers, though the comments were concentrated mainly on the coach: 'Isn't it lovely! Isn't it gorgeous!' Debate centred on who was who. Typical snatches of dialogue as the procession passed a point in Regent Street:

Woman:	'No, not yet. I think the Duchess first.'
Another:	'That's the Queen.' Then, disappointed, 'No.'
	'That's Queen Mary.'
	'That's Princess Marina.'
	'Princess Royal, that is.'
	'The Queen of Norway.'
	'I saw Marina.'
	'I'm sure Queen Mary's next.'
	'Hullo, George, boy. Well, Marina!'
	'This is Queen Mary's coach next.'
	'There are the Princesses. Aren't they sweet?'
	'They're well trained.'
	'After the King comes the Duke of Gloucester.'
	'That one's a piebald.'
	'I saw Queen Mary. Did you?' 'Yes.'
	'The two Dukes at the back, of course, being on horseback.'
	'Yes, I saw them.'
	'That's the end.'
	'That's that.'

	'That's the tail-end of it now.'
	'Two more coming.'
	'Black Maria coming now.'
	'It's best to follow the crowd.'
Father to	'We've seen something we shall never
young daughter:	see again.'
Mother:	'She may; we shan't.'
Father:	'Well, I mean, she may not get the opportunity. We may not be this way again.'

Among those who actually watched the procession such remarks as the passing of George VI provoked were generally flattering – 'There's the right man for the job.' Champions of the Duke of Windsor stayed away or were discreetly silent. Around the country, though, there seems to have been a fair representation of those who hankered after Edward VIII. A hairdresser's mother in Nottingham listened to the service with tears pouring down her face, moaning '*Oh*, it ought to be Edward – it – it – it ought to be Edward!' 'My mother's a scream,' commented the hairdresser disloyally. A landlady in South London said: 'She wouldn't give a thank you to be there, not after the dirty trick they had played on the old Duke of Windsor.' A cinema operator in Scotland 'expressed the opinion that the King was in the hands of the clergy. Edward wouldn't stand for this so was kicked out.' A Cambridge tradesman who saw the procession on television* considered 'it just shows all this socialist nonsense up, doesn't it?' but argued repeatedly that the Windsors were as good as the rest of the family.

Whether the enthusiasm shown for Queen Mary and the Princesses represented an appreciation of family values or a sentimental reaction to the sight of two attractive children

---

* 60,000 viewers are believed to have watched the procession on television, which could be received up to sixty-three miles from the point of transmission (Ipswich being the most distant point covered).

in such formal circumstances can hardly be decided. Certainly the comments overheard do not suggest a very sophisticated response. 'Oh, aren't they lovely?' said most of the adults at a point on the Victoria Embankment. 'Aren't they sweet?' To a left-wing atheist in the crowd it seemed that the only sincere cheers were for the old Queen and her grand-daughters. To some extent the children must have provided light relief in what was otherwise an emotionally highly-charged occasion, in the same way as two army chaplains who got out of step and, 'glaring fiercely at each other, proceeded to do a fantastic little dance until the rhythm caught them up'.

Throughout the day the BBC was reporting on the procession and the service in the Abbey. Along the route broadcasts of the service produced broadly similar reactions: initial indifference; embarrassed half-attention – should one smoke? is it all right to eat a sandwich?; close concentration at the climactic moments. At Hyde Park Corner wireless reception was poor: 'The large number of wandering people distracted attention from the Crowning. On the words "His Majesty King George VI is acclaimed" there is a moment of indecision among the seat-holders – whether to stand up or not – and by all whether to take off hats or not. The seat-holders cheer first, then as the Abbey cheering comes through they stand up. About half the men in the general crowd raise or take off their hats. Two ice-cream boys push each other about in fun because one hasn't taken his hat off.' A little way off 'God Save the King' 'exercises a slow but finally compelling effect on the crowd. By the last line almost everyone is silent and standing still, the men with their hats off. They do not sing, but immediately after they give three cheers.'

By the evening the centre of London was a sorry sight. Drizzle throughout the day and innumerable feet had transformed the parks into muddy and litter-strewn bogs. In Soho, 'all the adults look weary and depressed – very few

61

have raincoats or umbrellas and the children by now are all being carried'. Piccadilly Circus was 'in the hands of a street gang who seem to be coping with several tons of paper, broken boxes, wrecked umbrellas, torn flags, hats – and mysteriously – one good silk stocking'. But there were also a host of young men and, still more, girls, 'who all seem to have enjoyed the show and are going to keep on enjoying it'.

The party was indeed far from over. With the police exercising a minimum of restraint the West End was given over to Bacchanalian revel, drunken and noisy certainly but good-tempered and with little in the way of vandalism. Outside Selfridges RAF men were dancing. Some people hopefully waved banners reading 'Washed in the Blood of the Lamb' and 'Repent, for the Day of Judgement is Nigh!' They were promptly festooned with rosettes and balloons, but the banner-bearers did not seem to mind. In Trafalgar Square a laughing policeman tried to stop people climbing the plinth of Nelson's column. He was rewarded with 'For he's a jolly good fellow', followed by 'Knees up Mother Brown' danced in a circle around him. In Piccadilly Circus a bell was being rung furiously and men were dancing with bare legs on a muddy spot by the barricaded statue of Eros. 'Doesn't it give you a terrific thrill walking across streets?' asked a woman. By Lyons' Corner House in Coventry Street a drunk woman was admiring the chocolates in the window. 'That's nice, isn't it?' Her daughter repeated the remark inanely. A man passed, beating an oven-tray; another man on top of a taxi. 'It's Coronation, so we've got to celebrate it, so whoopee!' said one young man to another, thus neatly encapsulating the spirit of the evening.

It was, of course, in front of Buckingham Palace that the crowds were thickest. There, however, things were more decorously conducted. 'Crowds dispersed in a most orderly fashion. Everything well organized, everyone in good humour,' noted one Mass Observer approvingly. The sobriety was unusual, the good humour not. Yet though the

King was cheered thunderously when he appeared on the balcony his speech that evening, broadcast over the whole processional route, was something of an anti-climax. 'That was lovely wasn't it?' said a middle-aged woman, 'he's gained in confidence a bit'; but most people hardly listened, complaining about the weather or worrying about their transport home. The national anthem took people by sur-

'*I know I'm not really an emperor – I just happen to like dressing up as one.*'

prise. It lasted longer than they expected. 'They twice began to put their hats on at the wrong place. Singing very half-hearted.' They had had enough.

The final image of the night comes from Gloucester Place. 'I am passed by a little middle-aged man very sozzled and straddled across the pavement staggering from one side to the other: sings at the top of his voice waving bowler hat in hand, "God Save the King" – words drawn out as long as they will bear.'

London is not Britain, nor the West End London. All over the British Isles the cities, towns and villages were conducting their private celebrations, sometimes so private that it is hard to trace any connection with the affair in the metropolis. At Prestwick a procession included the city dignitaries in top hats, decorated lorries representing the town's trade and history, two or three humorous tableaux, a young man on a velocipede, the Boys' Brigade Band, a model lighthouse on a lorry, but only the most cursory references to the Coronation. The master of ceremonies, introducing the pageant at a Lancashire village, devoted his remarks entirely to the village's ambition to become a non-county borough. To judge by the overheard conversation of a group of youths the pageant itself was equally detached from the events in London:

A youth	(seeing Father Time approach): 'Someone's wearing the sheet. Go on. All clap!'
Another:	'Deserted world this.'
	'Very good what we've seen so far.'
	'If we look like a lettuce will they let us in those seats?'
	'It's an invasion.'
	'Have a toffee.'
	'Ooh!'

As caveman and cavewoman squabble over large bone:

'What are they? I don't know.'

As prehistoric beasts appear:

'Didn't know there was ever anything here like that.'

'What are those?'

'Arabs?'

'I don't understand it.'

'They're Druids. We have it at school.'

'They ought to have someone telling us what it's all about.'

'Fancy 2/- for those seats, and they're damp too.'

'It's slow.'

'It's time we had something to eat.'

In a Suffolk village things were run on more patriotic lines. The local MP harangued a small crowd of rain-soaked villagers from the balcony of the castle. Beer was then drunk from Coronation mugs, but this was insufficient to raise dampened spirits. 'The one rollicking figure is Mrs S, a village woman of sixty-five or so, who has a Coronation scarf round her neck, another round her hat, an over-dress of crinkled paper in red, white and blue panels. All round her large umbrella are hung Coronation pompoms.' Guns were heard in the distance and the health of the King was drunk. The wife of the MP, with a look of relief, pronounced in ringing tones: 'Well, he's crowned, and that's all that matters.'

Street parties proliferated in the provincial towns and cities as much as in the suburbs of London. In the better-class areas of Birmingham 70 to 80% of people were wearing paper hats and street games were organized – three-legged races, balloons, dancing to pianos on pavements. Some streets put ropes across both ends so as to protect their revels from intruders. After tea at Balls Park, Hertford, the children began to throw plates, cups and saucers. Practically everything was smashed and they finished by tearing up the tablecloths.

'The story of Birmingham's demonstration of loyalty to the King and Queen at their crowning,' proclaimed the *Birmingham Post*, 'is one that will be told and retold with

pride in years to come. This was a day, it will be said, when
England's second city showed to the last man, woman and
child, its devotion to the Throne and its pride in the Empire.'

There are indeed quite enough reports from people who
passed through 'decorated streets among crowds who without exception seemed to be smiling' to suggest that Birmingham did indeed celebrate with fervour and much pleasure.
Yet in the same city a group were discussing some acquaint-
ances who had gone to London to see the procession.

'Christ!' said a young man. 'Half of 'em never seen a thing!'

'What about the old girl who got there yesterday afternoon?' asked a plump young man with a red face.

'Let 'em sit up as wants to,' said an old man. 'I wouldn't.
Ought to have a gold medal. She'll wonder why she's got
the 'flu next week. After all, he's only a human being.'

'You've said it,' said a young man wearing an enormous
rosette.

'I had to stand eight hours to see the old King lying in
state,' said the plump one.

'It'd have to be more than one king for me,' said the old
man. 'When you got to him you only saw a union jack over
him.'

'That's it. That's just about it,' agreed the plump one.

Hardly strong meat to a republican, but at variance with
the vision of happy, smiling faces and full-blooded ardour.

Two people, of course, could survey the same scene and
emerge with radically different impressions. An Observer
in Glasgow was much struck by the good nature and jollity
of all concerned, yet another, in much the same part of the
city, saw only 'crowds running about with no apparent aim
or purpose. There are a great many drunks. Women in
shawls and girls are rubbing their faces with "make-up"
that is used for branding cattle in the markets. Streaked
with blue and red they look like Maoris, or painted savages
in a war dance. They seem capable of anything. Small
gangs in side streets are lighting fires that may become

definitely dangerous in congested areas like these. The atmosphere is electric. The people seem to feel that tonight the police are powerless. They can do what they like.'

Yet though the atmosphere might sometimes turn sour, cynicism creep in, violence erupt, the community of views between all those who celebrated the Coronation was indeed astonishing. Directly anti-monarchist remarks were so rarely reported, even from areas where unemployment was high and resentment of authority notorious, that they are immediately memorable. One of the few examples came from the smiling city of Birmingham; a drunken ex-soldier who boasted of the medals he had won fighting for England. He put his hand on the head of a passing child. 'This little girl,' he said, 'is as good as the woman who was crowned Queen today. Ain't she?' He gave the Observer a baleful look, then continued, 'She's as good as royalty, the little duck. I fought for England, for the *people* of England! Not royalty!'

No doubt the republicans sensibly stayed at home, yet one of the most difficult achievements was wholly to escape the Coronation. A keen cyclist from South Norwood decided to get away from it all in a long spin through the deserted roads on the Kent-Sussex border. 'Every habitation decorated,' he reported, 'and from every cottage came the sound of cheering. Very few people about in fields or gardens – evidently all listening to the broadcast commentary. At each village there were celebrations in the open air – dancing, sports, brass bands. Somehow the countryside seemed to purify even Coronation emotionalism of its unhealthy fever. It was spontaneous merry-making that we saw, probably little changed from what it was centuries ago.'

'Unhealthy fever'? To others the merry-making in the cities seemed spontaneous enough, and the fever positively benign. Certainly it proved singularly infectious and those who resisted it were often too sick themselves to have any chance of succumbing. 'Me and Jane never stirred out all day,' recorded an old age pensioner. 'It wasn't fit. We didn't even go to t' pictures. And my poor feet was awful, awful!'

The evidence of the Mass Observation Archive furnishes no great surprises. People on the whole behaved as they might have been expected to do. Their participation in the Coronation was not as whole-hearted as the professional romantics would have had one believe, yet certainly far more enthusiastic than the cynic would find it easy to accept. Certain points seem irrefutable. Very nearly the entire adult population was aware of the Coronation and a vast majority was to some extent involved in its celebration. Of these some at least were initially hostile, yet when it came to the point most of these were pleased to be participating. A genuine sense of common interest developed, transcending temporarily barriers of geography or social class. The Briton felt more conscious of being such and more proud of his nationality than had been the case for many years. He had been moved and excited by the Coronation, even though he may not have been very clear what excited him or what was the significance of the ceremonial which caused it. A deep, atavistic chord had been touched and the experience had been stimulating – even, for some, ennobling.

How much of all this lasted is another problem, and one even less susceptible to scientific solution. For the monarch, however, the effect did endure. After the abdication crisis sensible people well disposed towards the royal family were seriously debating whether Britain could survive without becoming a republic. After the Coronation such debate would have seemed as futile and as academic as during the palmy days of King George V. The Coronation did not cause this *volte face* but it contributed largely to the change of atmosphere in which the *volte face* could occur. The British people felt more affectionate towards the King and Queen and, above all, far more committed to them. For the monarchy, that was the real point of the Coronation.

CHAPTER THREE

The Monarchy at War

The last resort of an unpopular dictator is traditionally to conjure up some threat from outside the country which will rally all the patriots behind him. On the same analogy, it might be expected that the extreme perils of war would rally the nation behind the symbol of its nationhood; pre-eminently, in Britain, the monarchy. Hard evidence is difficult to come by – nobody conducted public opinion polls in the middle of the war to establish whether the royal family meant less or more to its subjects than at other times – yet such indications as there are suggest that the facts were rather different.

The reactions to various speeches by the King of those who kept diaries for Mass Observation throughout the war provide an interesting barometer of public opinion.[1] War was declared on 3 September 1939, and that evening the King addressed his people. It should have been the climactic moment of a memorable day, yet of the sixty-one male diarists only eleven mentioned the royal speech, of the fifty-five women only thirteen. Almost without exception the diarists had listened to the Prime Minister earlier in the day and commented on his speech. Of those who did listen to the King none referred to the content of his speech while several wrote of the stammer which made his public speaking so painful to all concerned. 'Poor man!' 'It's a shame!' 'He's very courageous to do it,' 'Bless him!' were the typical remarks of a family in Sidcup, while a republican librarian from Bristol was moved to claim, 'He said it very nicely.'

References to the national anthem which was played at the end of the King's speech illustrate the changing pattern of behaviour between then and the present day. A forty-seven-year-old journalist from Manchester noted, 'we all stood rigidly to attention, looking and perhaps feeling rather foolish in the small low-ceilinged lounge'; a nineteen-year-old student 'stood up without hesitation or embarrassment'; while a spinster in Essex 'stood up for "God Save the King" and my little dog got out of her basket and stood beside me'. One of the few deviants, an actress from Crowfoot, rushed to turn off the radio before the music began, thus betraying as much consciousness of the anthem's potency as those who stood at attention.

20·7% of diarists listened to the speech on 3 September;[2] for the Christmas Day speech of 1939 the proportion was a very similar 22·7%.[3] From then on the trend was generally downwards: 14·5% for the Empire Day speech in 1940; 12% for the Christmas speech in 1940, 9·3% in 1941, a resurgence to 16% in 1942, 9% again in 1943, 8% in 1944. The statistical base was extremely narrow, the approach of the diarists tended to be more sceptical and left-wing than was true of the generality of the nation, but the trend is still significant.

What did not differ was the emphasis on the delivery rather than the content. As a child of nine or ten I can remember listening to those royal broadcasts, willing the King to get through the trickier passages without a breakdown. I see now that I was far from being alone. His problem won him much sympathy. 'We felt terribly sorry for the poor man,' wrote a student in December 1939. 'It's a shame to make him speak with his disability. We could have wept at his stumbles.' 'Poor chap,' commented a London housewife of the same speech, 'he tackles it manfully but it must be a horrible ordeal.'

When the matter of the speech *did* earn attention the judgement varied sharply. 'Dreary stuff,' wrote a Gateshead woman of the speech in September 1940 which announced the introduction of the George Cross. 'We know it by heart already. Why get the poor lad up to speak? One likes him alright, but hasn't time for slow stuff.' An electrician from Farnborough was 'bored by the platitudes'. Yet a London housewife thought it '. . . a very good speech. Ought to pep up the Empire,' while a Cheshire woman of twenty-eight described it as 'splendid, his delivery very much better'. On the whole women were more enthusiastic about what he said and more appreciative of the effort he made in saying it.[4]

It is instructive to compare these entries with the comparable diary entries for Churchill's speeches. Not every diarist was a fan of the Prime Minister's, but virtually all of them listened whenever he spoke and commented on what he said. In this fact lies one of the causes for the partial eclipse of the monarch. The people needed a heroic figure who would excite and inspire them; temperamentally and physically George VI was unable to fill this need, while Churchill did so to perfection. Churchill's grandiloquent oratory, flamboyant gestures and facile if sincere emotionalism delighted and fulfilled the British people. They were alien to the repertoire of the King. Professor Rose in his valuable and stimulating study *The Monarchy in Contemporary British Culture*, citing de Gaulle, Hitler, Ataturk as examples, has suggested that. 'The charismatic figure who fills an institutional void, using his *persona* to substitute for constitutional forms of authority, is normally a commoner.'[5] It is not necessary to look far to find exceptions to this rule, but the odds against any given monarch having the will and the personality to play the role must be considerable. George VI had neither.

A survey conducted for Mass Observation shows the same swelling indifference.[6] In a cinema it was noted that in thirty-eight newsreels screened between the outbreak of war and January 1940 the royal family appeared thirty-six times and were applauded thirteen times. In the following six months the number of appearances declined steeply and the ratio of applause more steeply still.

In November 1940 seventy-nine Durham schoolchildren were asked to write down what they had particularly noticed in the newspapers the previous week. In all, twenty-four items were mentioned; there were sixty-three references to the death of Chamberlain, but only one girl wrote of a tour of the local air-raid shelters by the King and Queen, even though this had been prominently reported. 'I should think they're quite nice people,' remarked a middle-class man of twenty in July 1940, 'quite harmless, but redundant – is that the word? – unnecessary. I'm not very interested in them.' 'People simply aren't interested in them,' said another man. 'They don't dislike them, or anything – they just don't think about them.' It seemed almost as if the royal family had been put away with other peacetime luxuries; to be resurrected, perhaps, when there was more time for in-essentials. 'I think it's all a bit silly – kings and queens in wartime,' said a working-class woman of forty-five. 'I don't think they're wanted. All them things are all right in peace-time – we like to have ceremonies and royal robes – but now it's up to us all, not kings and queens.' As the war became more fierce, the possibility of defeat more real, so the frills became unwanted, even offensive. 'Nobody mentions "King and Country", "The Crown", "Homeland", etc. etc.,' noted a postman from Bromley. 'I can't record any remarks including the word "glorious" used in the sense of "glorious attack . . ." etc.'

Indifference was one thing, but a note of disaffection became more apparent as the strains of war began to tell. Criticism centred on the belief that the royal family still lived in comparative luxury if not security and was protected from the worst tribulations of wartime existence. 'It's all very well for them,' said a London housewife from Kensington who had been bombed out for the second time, 'traipsing around saying how their hearts bleed for us and they share all our sufferings, and then going home to a roaring fire in one of their six houses.' When in his speech on VE Day the King spoke of having lived through the bombing with his people, a seventy-four-year-old woman from Orpington 'thought of those Lewisham women who told the Queen to go away because she could not understand their lives, she had other homes to go to'.

*'I was given to understand it was just
an honorary rank.'*

The death of the Duke of Kent in a plane crash illustrated well how genuine sympathy could be tinged with a jaundiced hue.[7] A typical dialogue between two women in a Leeds bus queue ran as follows:

'Fancy the Duke of Kent being killed. Isn't it sad?'

'Well, royalty have as much right to be killed in the war as other folk.'

'That's not the way to talk, his wife and children will miss him the same as anyone else.'

'That may be, but they don't have to worry about who is going to keep them like we should have to do.'

'That's nothing to do with it. Everyone misses their own, it's a cruel way to look at it, you wouldn't talk like that if the Duke of Kent had been your husband.'

'Somehow you feel that such people should be immune,' wrote a civil servant from Morecambe, and many people seem genuinely to have felt a thrill of horror at such a fate befalling a member of the royal family. Yet the spinster from Peterborough seems to have spoken for a substantial part of the British people when she added the bitter comment: 'She won't have to work to keep those children. *We* will.'

It has already been suggested that the traditional association of royalty with good works or technical triumphs – the opening of hospitals, the launching of ships – fosters a subliminal belief that the royal visitors are connected with or even in some way responsible for the achievement. If there is any truth in this, in wartime the converse must be true. The King and Queen were assiduous in their visits to bombed cities; the most common image evoked by those who recollect the wartime monarchy is of a slight, sad figure clambering over a pile of rubble. Inevitably the King came to be associated with destruction and doom: the visits might improve the morale of the victims, probably of the nation too, but cumulatively they contributed to a pattern of melancholy and dismay. Sometimes, even, he seemed to be a harbinger of evil. 'I heard at lunch that the King seems to have visited a neighbouring town yesterday which was treated to its first air raid in two weeks last night. Was it a coincidence?' asked a diarist who lived near Colchester in October 1940. The heaviest blitz on Plymouth

came on 20 and 21 March 1941 – the nights directly following a well-publicized royal visit.

In December 1940, when Southampton was reeling,
virtually leaderless, after several nights of devastating blitz,
King George VI arrived to inspect the damage and hearten
the citizens. 'Excited multitudes lined the wintry streets,'
wrote an equally excited local historian. What followed was
a 'fervent demonstration of love, loyalty and enthusiasm
as in days gone by reserved for the occasion of an Elizabethan
triumph'.[8] In fact the royal party arrived unannounced and
passed virtually unnoticed. Most of the inhabitants heard of
the visit on the radio that night and their reaction was
unenthusiastic when their opinions were canvassed the
following morning. 'I suppose they do a certain amount of
good coming round but I wish they'd give me a new house,'
was one of the more friendly comments, while the male view
was generally that they had no time for that sort of fuss –
'too busy cleaning up and one thing and another'.[9]

This is to present only the negative side of the picture.
The failure of the royal family in wartime, insofar as they
can be said to have failed at all, existed only in relation to
the role which those who had watched the Coronation
might have expected them to play and the sort of personal
success achieved by Winston Churchill. For many, perhaps
most of King George VI's subjects, the preceding paragraphs
would provide an unrecognizable parody of what to them
had been a signally important contribution to Britain's
victory.

The bombing of Buckingham Palace in September 1940
showed how the attitudes differed. A fifty-year-old man from
Essex took the line: 'What if the King and Queen do get
killed? They're only people like us. Why should they have
special precautions taken?' Most of those who commented,
however, took a more robustly loyal stance. 'What a wicked
thing to do!' said a woman clerk of twenty-five. 'If they
hurt the King or Queen or the Princesses we'd be so mad
we'd blast every German out of existence.' 'If it's deliberate,

I'm bloody annoyed about it,' commented the managing director of a textile firm. 'The King and Queen are nice people, and it's hitting below the belt to single them out.'[10]

Yet the indignation was often mixed with a certain satisfaction, the satisfaction the Queen herself felt when she remarked: 'I'm glad we've been bombed. It makes me feel I can look the East End in the face.'[11] A socialist assistant librarian was voicing the same sentiment, though starting from different premises, when he said that bombing the East End had caused untold misery and could easily have led to discontent and disunion, 'but with the King bombed we are once again united in our cause'. The fact that, even though their life might be more comfortable, the royal family conspicuously shared their people's perils and that the King worked as hard as any of his subjects undoubtedly contributed to a sense of common purpose and common effort. 'They say they've sent the little Princesses to Canada, but I can't believe they'd do such a thing,' was a contemporary comment.[12] The scepticism was justified: the Princesses stayed in Britain. 'All the other countries have gone to pieces – and why? Because they didn't have a popular King to bind the country together. I think they give a feeling of national unity . . .'[13] The apparition of foreign royalties arriving in London in flight from the German invader inevitably led to speculation whether the British might not be similarly deserted, but few doubted that the King would stick it out to the last minute or beyond – 'You won't find George quitting without a good reason, I'm sure of that!'[14]

Though the King might not inspire by stirring oratory or win hearts by the warmth of his personality the totality of his dedication could never be doubted. He was visibly wearing himself out by his efforts in the national cause. In Barrow, in May 1940, a fifty-year-old working-class woman 'on every side heard pitying remarks about the worn and tired looks of the King. He looks far from being a strong man and it must be weary to be a King . . .'[15] It was not so much the well-publicized economies – the shallow baths, the dimmed lights – as the physical proof which his presence presented that he was single-minded and considered no sacrifice too great if it contributed to final victory. He was a walking personification of the nation's sense of duty. 'The King and Queen set a wonderful example to the whole country, though the King has a terrible job,' was praise which many of those least enthused by the monarch would have admitted was well earned.

There were many too to attest that the visits constantly paid to the blitzed cities did do much to raise morale and re-establish a sense of purpose. A survivor of the Coventry blitz recorded years later: 'We suddenly felt that if the King was there everything was all right and the rest of England was behind us.'[16] On a visit to Portsmouth the King and Queen were told of a woman who had been bombed out of two houses and was now inadequately housed in a third. They asked to see her. The detective knocked on the door and a woman with a baby in her arms came out:

'We heard of your misfortune,' began the Queen. 'May we come in and talk to you?' The woman gaped incredulously at this apparition. 'The King and I would so much like to bring you such comfort as we can, and to hear your story.'

'Oh, do come in,' said the woman, still doubtful of her visitors' identity.

'We understand this is your third home,' said the King.

'That's right. He burned us out of one and he flooded us out of another, but he'll never get us out of here!'[17]

Unless this Portsmouth woman was most exceptional this direct contact with royalty would have been one of the high spots of her life and, if she is still alive, will remain one of her most cherished memories. Again and again one finds that the most tenuous brush with royalty is lovingly recorded – indeed, remains vivid in the mind of those who in principle have no use for the institution. A nurse from Midlothian writes that 'she had just been photographed beside the Queen when the Queen visited her canteen'; a woman showed one of the Mass Observation diarists 'a photo of her husband in uniform standing beside the Queen'; when the Duke of Kent was killed a young garage assistant in King's Lynn wrote that he felt very sorry 'and feel it more as I saw him looking so nice in Lynn three weeks ago'; a Glasgow journalist was the more moved because he had a friend who had met the Duke several times.[18] Contact with royalty had a talismanic effect and though the papers may have overrated the mass impact on the crowds the individual was undoubtedly inspired and heartened. In his diary the King commented: 'I feel that this kind of visit does do good at such a moment and it is one of my main jobs in life to help others when I can be useful to them.'[19] Perhaps the King's principal contribution to national unity was that he persuaded all but the most sceptical of his subjects that this was indeed his personal philosophy.

There were newspapers and propagandists who tried to inflate the achievement of the royal family above its real and considerable value. 'The King and Queen visited us in Liverpool on Wednesday,' recorded a shipping-clerk, 'but as they came unannounced very few people saw them. I was talking on the phone yesterday and my friend told me that they were then visiting Lancaster, but as nobody was expecting them, very few people were congregated about. Last night the wireless announced that the crowds [in both cities] were so great that their car had to go at walking-pace. One of us is wrong.'[20]

Similar incidents are too common to leave much doubt that over-enthusiastic reporting was at fault. Perhaps the truest comment on the role of the royal family in wartime comes from a young private soldier from a working-class family who gropingly tried to set out his thoughts to a Mass Observer in October 1940:

I'd never get half hysterical over them like what some do. I'm afraid I'm not at all that patriotic. When a man like me's fighting for 'is country, as they say, it's not the King and Queen 'e's fighting for, it's England. Well, that goes

for me at any rate, and I suppose that it goes for the rest
of the boys on the 'ole, from what I've seen . . . After all,
they're not Gods, they're just human beings like us. Well,
I think they are marvellous people and all that, they
represent the best type of the upper class and so on, and
they do a damn awful job extremely well, give 'em that.
They're only – now what's the word I want – what I
mean, they only *represent* what we're really fighting for,
which is our country. They're just figure-heads, not the
real thing . . .

CHAPTER FOUR

Wedding and Funeral

The years between the end of the war and the death of King George VI in February 1952 were not happy ones for Britain. The euphoria of victory was swiftly dissipated and paying the bills of war proved painful and protracted. The brave new world promised by the politicians obstinately failed to materialize, austerity grew more rather than less oppressive without even the stimulus of national danger to make it tolerable.

What role should the royal family play at such a period? The phenomenal success of the American musical *Oklahoma*, brimful with colour and warmth, showed how the British people craved for spectacle. Should the monarchy seek to meet this hunger by a conspicuous return to the lavish pageantry of before the war? Such a role would hardly have suited the King, as grey and battered as any of his subjects. He saw his function as being to preach by personal example the qualities of restraint and self-discipline. Nor were the British people in a mood to welcome any ostentatious extravagance in high places. The national mood was strikingly demonstrated in May 1947. The King and Queen set off on a lengthy and inevitably expensive tour of Southern Africa. An opinion poll showed that only 29% of those interviewed actively approved the tour, mainly in the belief that it would strengthen the bonds of Empire.[1] Slightly more, 32%, actually disapproved, on the grounds that the visit served no useful purpose, that it was just a holiday in disguise, and that it was wrong for the royal family to indulge in expensive junketings when people at home were so badly off. The remainder had no pronounced views about the tour one way or the other.

Later that same year, however, came evidence that the doings of the royal family could still kindle excitement and that the taste for pageantry was not dead. 'Grand news this morning about Princess Elizabeth's engagement,' recorded a female civil servant from Morecambe. 'Of course it had been expected for some time . . . but it seems no less exciting when it is officially announced. I should like to have been among the crowd in the Mall this evening to see them on the balcony.' The engagement, wrote a woman diarist, 'is one of those pleasant and happy events which no one can object to, and which the British people invariably love'. A housewife from Otley did object, on the grounds that Prince Philip was 'a relation and a Glucksberg at that', and found some support, as from a forty-year-old middle-class man who felt terrible because Elizabeth was marrying a Greek. 'With Attlee and Bevin being Jews, England will soon be ruled by a lot of foreigners.' Such complaints were rare, however, and the housewife was on safer ground when she added that Philip seemed 'a nice enough man even if not over-bright'. The belief that the Prince was amiable but dim seemed to have been widespread: 'though not brilliant he will doubtless fit very well into the semi-background of court life,' was another diarist's somewhat patronizing comment.

It would have been possible to pitch the affair in a minor key, in keeping with the circumstances of the country, but instead it was decided to celebrate the marriage with traditional vigour – 'England's answer to *Oklahoma*', as a provincial leader-writer somewhat ambiguously described it. Inevitably this led to recriminations. 'I think it's a damned waste of money,' said a lower-middle-class woman of thirty. 'I don't see why she should have everything when there are so many who have to make do with makeshift weddings and others can't get married at all because they have no home to go to.' A poll taken some months before the event tested reactions to the report that Princess Elizabeth's wedding dress would take 300 clothing coupons on the existing ration-scale and cost £1200.[2] Of those asked 37% thought this reasonable, 36% did not; men not surprisingly were far more critical than women. 'I'm very pleased. Everything is so dull now,' said a working-class woman of twenty-five. A thirty-five-year-old labourer who voted Labour had no time for the royal family: 'They have outlived their useful-ness. But I think myself that if you have got to have Royalty they may as well have everything to do with the wedding in a truly royal fashion.' In this attitude he was exceptional: nearly half the Labour voters of all sexes and a marked majority of the males condemned the extravagance of the occasion.

Even four months before the wedding it was virtually impossible not to know about it: of 112 people asked only one, a road-sweeper in Bloomsbury, admitted total ignorance. Of the others, however, over 40% professed indifference: 'Feel? What should I feel?' 'I don't care, it doesn't affect me,' 'It's not my business, it's up to them,' were typical comments, while even among those who were in favour such detached remarks as 'I don't mind' or 'I suppose she has to be married, it's very necessary,' were not uncommon.

At this point the royal family could have been forgiven for wondering whether their decision to celebrate the wedding in style was the right one. The Camden Town First Branch of the Amalgamated Society of Woodworkers struck a gloomy note. 'It wishes to remind you,' the wood-workers told the King, 'that any banqueting and display of wealth will be an insult to the British people at the present time.' Furthermore, they continued menacingly, 'should you declare the wedding day a public holiday you will have a word beforehand with the London Master Builders Associa-tion to ensure that we are paid for it'.[3] To the Mayor of Winchester was directed a long tirade against the monarchy which ended succinctly: 'Best wishes to you from the lawful Queen of England, commonly known as E. M. Ottewall.'[4]

It seems a feature of royal occasions that the initial public reaction should be one of indifference tinged with disapproval but that, as the date approaches, so enthusiasm waxes. Between a poll in July and another in October the proportion of those who actively approved of the marriage rose from 40 to 60%.[5] A large number of people still felt the arrangements were on too lavish a scale, but another poll of 5 November, a fortnight before the wedding, showed that the proportion had dropped to 29%.[6] It would have been astonishing if the proportion had not been dramatically smaller on the day itself.

On the wedding day it proved hard indeed to remain remote from the proceedings. In a typical provincial office all talk was of the royal family. A wireless set was put on upstairs: 'We couldn't get into the room and just joined the crowd clustered outside the room.' In a Scottish factory work stopped almost entirely: 'They may just have been glad of the break,' said a manager dubiously, 'but they certainly *seemed* enthusiastic enough.' Next day a socialist Mass Observer in Manchester tried to buy a newspaper. 'I found every paper sold. I was astonished, but was told the reason was that people wanted to see the pictures of the Royal Wedding. I think there is no doubt that the Royal Family is very popular. Were they to disappear, the people would be very upset.'

As always one asks oneself how far this enthusiasm was genuine and spontaneous, how far a spurious creation of the media. Is there indeed such a thing as 'spurious' enthusiasm; is it not genuine by the mere fact of its existence, irrespective of the forces that fomented it? To most Observers who commented the enthusiasm seemed real enough. 'The feeling is genuine,' wrote a woman from Leatherhead, 'a delighted sort of family feeling. I always get it when watching any royal do.' To some, indeed, it seemed that the mood was being carried too far. 'I think people who slept on pavements in the cold and wet are crazy,' wrote a housewife from Sheffield, balefully predicting that cases of pneumonia would develop over the week-end.

It was the romance, the fairy-tale element which appealed to some Observers. 'All of us are hungry for colour, romance and adventure. Today's ceremony symbolizes some sort of dormant form of perfection alive in the breast of every average – well – woman at least.' Others felt that the wedding emphasized the familial element of British royalty. To these people the prime significance of the monarchy in contemporary society was that it incarnated the values of the traditional family: decency, responsibility, solidarity; '. . . we demand some sort of symbol of what is perhaps, emotionally, the most important part of our way of life – the family.' Yet the reaction most often expressed was one of patriotism, almost chauvinism. As the power of Britain waned so pride grew in the royal family as something which was uniquely ours and which no country could match. 'I wonder what foreigners would think of our loyal greetings to the crown,' speculated a male Observer from SE 26. 'I expect that some of the royal visitors would feel jealous and wonder whether they would get the same kind of greeting in their own countries?' It was a sentiment that was to grow in stridence over the next twenty-five years.

With the marriage between Princess Elizabeth and Prince Philip the monarchy gained a new and incomparably brighter focus of attention. The King was in no sense forgotten – his ever-conscientious attention to duty alone made this impossible – but in a curious way he was written off. Elizabeth was the future; the petering-out of her father's reign – for few believed he could have many years to live – was an interlude to be lived through as gracefully as possible. Nobody *wanted* the King dead, but there were many who looked forward to a new reign as heralding a brighter, more successful Britain. Yet in spite of the King's continual poor health and a recent severe illness, the public assumed that he was on the mend when his daughter left on a protracted trip to Australia by way of Africa early in 1952. His sudden death some time in the night of 5–6 February took the nation by surprise.

Shock, out of all proportion to what might have been expected at the death of a man who personally was unknown to almost all those who heard the news, was the most common reaction. 'Can't believe it,' muttered a working-class woman of twenty-five. 'I didn't know him, never seen him or any of the royal family, but it's such a shock.' She felt 'ever so queer' and had to rush from her place of work for fear of being sick. 'Very sad, really sad,' said a labourer of forty-five. 'Died in his sleep? It's a shock to everyone. Come on us sudden.' A forty-year-old woman in a country village found it '. . . a great shock. My husband poured himself out a brandy and I said pour one out for me. You really felt as though you wanted it, it was such a shock. All I can say is, thank goodness we've still got Churchill.'

Of course the grief which even the most loyal of royalists experienced could not compare in intensity or duration with the feelings of someone who has lost a spouse or child; if only because their day-to-day life was only superficially disturbed. Yet it was far stronger and far more personal than it would have been in the case of any other public figure of whatever eminence – or of a catastrophe involving people unknown and unseen. 'Oh, I think it's dreadful!' said a woman working in a department store. 'I'm terribly sorry. I feel as shocked as if it was someone belonging to me.' 'I feel rather lost,' said a carpenter of forty-five. 'Don't quite know what to think about it really. When I heard first of all I felt it was a personal loss as though some of my own people had died.'

It is interesting to contrast such reactions with those encountered at the death of Churchill. No one would have contested that Churchill was by far the greater man, nor that he had done more for his country, yet the note of personal regret was lacking. However much they admired Churchill, no one seemed to think that he was 'someone belonging to me'. The circumstances of their deaths were widely different.

George VI's opened the way to a brighter future, Churchill's severed the last link with glory passed. Yet it was the King's death which struck people as a cataclysm. It caused among his subjects not only a personal loss but also a sense of awe – a sense which owed little to George VI's personality and almost everything to his status. 'I mean, he's special, isn't he?' explained a pit-head worker in Durham. 'I mean, he's the King. It's different when the King dies, isn't it?'

Affection for George VI was felt across the nation. 'I think we all liked the King a great deal,' said an artisan of twenty-five. 'Never wanted to be King. Sacrificed practically everything for his country. I think if anybody died for his country it was the King.' Sympathy for a man who had obviously suffered greatly was a common reaction. 'I'm very sorry for the old boy. He's had a rotten life,' commented a chemist of fifty-five. 'I am sorry for the King and I love him very, very much,' said the assistant to a watch-repairer, male and twenty-five. Panegyrics after death are no rarity and must be viewed with scepticism, but there is a note of sincerity in such remarks. In a bar at Notting Hill Gate a morose drinker intoned: 'He's only shit and soil now like anyone else.' Two other customers promptly attacked him and he had to be hustled out at the back to save him from serious damage.

The fact that George VI was a king, not merely a notability, was marked by the way thoughts turned at once to his heir. 'My pity and concern went in a rush of sympathy to Princess Elizabeth whose youth dies at twenty-six,' wrote a female diarist from Barrow. 'Terrible responsibility for Elizabeth,' observed a labourer of forty-five. Of ninety-four people questioned at one street corner fourteen made some reference to Princess Elizabeth, only one to her mother, the Queen. Is it conceivable that the death of any other man in the world would have caused so much concern for his daughter, so little for his widow?

A woman of forty, walking down Regent Street, encapsulated many of the popular reactions. She saw a sign saying 'King Dead', but rejected the idea that it could be *her* king, and walked on, refusing to be seduced into buying an unwanted paper. Another woman asked: 'Is the King dead?' 'I can't make it out,' she replied. She went into a Lyons to have coffee and heard two people agreeing that it

was rotten for Princess Elizabeth. Still she would not accept that George VI was dead. 'There was an old girl sitting beside me at the table, a scruffy old thing, and she had a paper but she didn't say anything – didn't look across and say "frightful news" or anything like that.' When she went out there were crowds around a news-vendor and she joined the queue. The vendor was 'almost paralysed with the unusualness of it, and nobody liked to push or shove, every-body was very polite which meant he didn't have to hurry and he was almost too slow . . .' At last she got her paper. 'Terrible news,' called out the news-vendor at the next corner. 'When I read it I was not very stunned, it was not until the afternoon that I realized how awful it was, the more you thought of it . . .'

The news of the King's death led to a revival of traditional patriotic attitudes. A plumber and his family from the Midlands found themselves standing rigidly to attention for the national anthem – 'something I can't remember doing since before the war'. At a school in the South of England the boys were ordered to assemble in the hall. They found the masters in black gowns, the Roll of Honour draped with the Union Jack. The headmaster mounted the platform and:

> In a voice filled with emotion, began, 'I have a most solemn and grave announcement to make to the school. The King is dead.' A hush descended, all the coughing and sneezing stopped as the announcement was made. The headmaster continued:
>
> 'I have assembled you here in order to send on your behalf and in the name of the school a message of con-dolence to the Queen. We will, in honour of the King, observe a moment's silence, after which we shall say the Lord's prayer as we are all members of one united family . . .'
>
> The Head Boy walked to the railings of the platform and said: 'Long Live the Queen!' The assembly termi-nated after the organ had played 'God Save the Queen'.

One of the more striking features of this vignette is the speed at which the Queen became the focus of attention. '*Le roi est mort, vive le roi,*' is a principle deeply ingrained in people's consciousness. Charles II learnt of his father's execution when a courtier addressed him as 'Your Majesty'. The fact that the succession was automatic and instantaneous was of real importance in those days when an interregnum would cause danger for the State; in the twentieth century it has lost practical significance but none of its ritual force. The feeling that there has been no break, that the throne is always occupied, is both a reassurance and a source of gratification to all those who have traditional instincts. At moments like this it becomes clear that such people comprise an overwhelming majority of the British people.

But though the King had been supplanted he must still depart with suitable ritual. Many thousands queued all night in rain and sometimes snow to file past the coffin in Westminster Hall. Those who were not able or did not wish to make the gesture regarded those who did with a curious mixture of approval, derision and even envy. A group discussed the phenomenon in the waiting-room of Haslemere Station:

A (A male artisan of fifty-odd): 'Wouldn't fancy lining up on a night like this to see the coffin!'

B (The Mass Observer): 'Is that what they're doing?'

A: '50,000 been through by 6.30 so the BBC says.'

B: 'Did they wait all night?'

A: 'Some of them did, so it says.'

B: 'I don't know why people should wait all night to see the coffin, though.'

A: 'No. Do you know, I saw the television of it yesterday? There was children and babes in arms – all in tears – just through the waiting! Well, *I* wouldn't! I don't mind queueing to see a good football match but not to see a coffin.'

C (A middle-class man of sixty): 'They do it because it's reality to them. They feel that it is *their* loss.'

B: 'I wonder if it isn't just sensationalism with some people.'

A: 'It was different with George V. His four sons stood at each side of the coffin. There was something to see then.'

Few of those who actually made the effort seem to have felt that their discomfort was inadequately rewarded. A little group spent more than eleven hours shuffling towards Westminster Hall. It consisted of a local council official and his wife (D and E), the latter of whom made surreptitious notes of the conversation, a seventy-year-old working-class woman (F), a sixteen-year-old boy (G) and his forty-year-old aunt (H) who seemed to be a widow eking out a pension by acting as part-time charlady (or perhaps, D thought, as a prostitute). The group were strangers at first but propinquity and shared tea and coffee broke down the barriers. It was notable that while crowds waiting all night for Coronations or similar ceremonies tried to sustain morale with songs and jokes, those queueing for the Lying-in-State felt anything of the sort would be out of place. Muted conversation with perhaps an occasional *sotto voce* laugh or exclamation was the most the crowd allowed itself.

At about 11 p.m. a particularly chilling gust of wind led D to speculate on why they were all submitting themselves to such torment when they could have been snug at home.

F: 'Well, it's the King, ain't it? Wouldn't do it for anyone else, mind you.'

E: 'But did you stay out all night before the Coronation?'

F: 'Wasn't in London then, but wouldn't have anyway. That's different, isn't it? I mean, a king dying – that's a thing, isn't it?'

H: 'Oh, I'd have done it for the Coronation. Will do too when the time comes. I never miss a royal occasion, not if I can manage it, like.'

E: 'But what do you do it for? You don't really see very much and you could read all about it and see the pictures in the papers next day. Why does your nephew want to spend all night here? What do *you* get out of it, Bill?'

G: 'Well, I don't really know. It's sort of different to actually be here, isn't it? I'll probably never see another king buried.'

H: 'It's all very well for you to talk. You're here too, aren't you?'

E: 'Yes, and I don't quite know why. I think, like Bill, I thought I'd never get another chance.'

D: 'It's not that. He's *my* King and I want to say good-bye to him, just as I would if he was a member of my family.'

F (breaking in eagerly): 'Yes, that's right. Same as if he was a father, really.'

H: 'We couldn't let him go just like he was anyone else. He was the King.'

F: 'Yes, it's different, ain't it?'

Overt signs of mourning were plentiful in London, less so in the provinces. As with other royal occasions public participation started modestly but worked up to a crescendo on the day itself. In High Street, Kensington, on the day of the funeral, fifty-nine out of ninety-seven shops were closed, at least for the hours of the processional service. Seventy-six showed some signs of mourning, ranging from a hair-dresser's adorned with a few perfunctory strips of black paper to a shoe shop which scrapped an entire window display to replace it by a large portrait of the King set in a giant wreath and surmounted by a scroll reading: 'In memory of King George VI, the well-beloved.' Taste occasionally wavered in such displays: a draper's shop in Kingston framed a photograph of the late monarch in swags of black bras, briefs and slips. All theatres and cinemas were closed throughout the capital.

The situation was different the farther one got from London. In Havant, a small town in Hampshire, little mourning was to be seen in the shops. 'Nothing's been done here so far,' reported the owner of a grocery store. 'But I must say I did feel a bit conspicuous when I went to put some bright red tins in the window this morning. It didn't seem quite the thing somehow.' In central Manchester the larger stores made quite a display of mourning but away from the city centre careful inspection was needed to find the occasional photograph or strip of crepe.

The Duke of Norfolk had asked that the country should observe three days of national mourning, that black arm-bands should be worn and bright clothes avoided. In the West End of London, on the day of the funeral at least, his wishes were largely respected: men wore black ties, women mainly black hats with black or mauve scarves. An industrial chemist of left-wing indications mentioned almost to his own surprise that he had worn a black tie for the first time since he left school in 1920. A failure to wear mourning could be as defiant a gesture in certain circles as a readiness to do so would appear in others; as a slavishly conformist undergraduate I can remember much anxious self-questioning as to what degree of solemnity would be appropriate to which set of friends. 'I think young people are extraordinary,' exclaimed a fifty-three-year-old civil servant. 'X is quite a decent fellow – educated – had a brilliant tie on – red and yellow. If you're asked to wear black it's only decency to do so. Anyone can afford a black tie. They all looked at me askance because I was wearing one.'

The two minutes' silence decreed for 2 p.m. on the day of the funeral provided still more acute polarization. It was much more generally observed than the exhortations about the use of mourning; no doubt because it involved less trouble and also because those who felt disinclined to conform could easily do so without running foul of the loyalists. Only the most principled or bloody-minded were prepared to flaunt their defiance of popular sentiment by walking and talking in public places. In the West End two men were taken up by the police to protect them from an

angry crowd. A middle-aged man of sixty went into Kensington Gardens to pass the two minutes' silence in peaceful
surroundings: 'A couple of dirty communists walked by
talking and laughing.'

But even the most ardent royalists were prepared to admit
that the BBC went a little far in injecting additional gloom
into the British scene. Sombre classical music, usually of a
religious nature, dominated the various programmes. 'Isn't
this wireless terrible?' exclaimed a working-class woman of
twenty-eight. 'A gentleman on the bus was talking to me –
I mean a real gentleman, not one of us – and he said the
King would have been furious.' Certainly the King would
have identified himself with the taste of the housewife who
complained: 'My brother-in-law likes it but my sister and I
can't stick it. We hates opera' – a reference presumably to
the religious oratorios which figured largely in the nation's
listening. People felt that things were already depressing
enough, without the radio seeking to heighten the mood.
'I think the BBC's disgraceful – too much of it,' said a
woman of sixty-five. 'Well, what I mean is, don't they think
of old folk, sick people, invalids? It's been terrible for them,
all this gloom. It's all been overdone.'

Much consolation was found in the fact that the death of
the King was mourned internationally as well as nationally.
A group was discussing the funeral in a town of southern
England:

A (A middle-class man of sixty-odd): 'Everyone feels
this as a personal loss. Not only us. The whole world
feels it.'

B (An artisan of fifty): 'You can tell that by the way
they're turning up to the funeral. Except the Belgians!
Even the King of Egypt's coming.'

C (A Mass Observer who happened to be present):
'What's happened about Belgium?'

B: 'He's not coming. He's sending a substitute. They
say he consulted with his father about it. Leopold the

traitor. Fancy consulting him!'

A: 'We can do without him. It's his loss, not ours.'

D (A woman of fifty-five): 'The Russian Ambassador is coming to the funeral.'

B: 'Is he? Is he! I'm glad to hear that.'

A: 'Well, he won't be able to say "No" this time.'

B (laughing): 'Ted Ray ought to hear that one. I say, Ted Ray ought to hear that!'

A: 'They're coming to the funeral from all over the world. It's a great tribute to him and it's a great tribute to us. Because George VI *is* us. He is us and we are him. He is the British people, all that is best in us, and we all know it.'

In these words A was articulating a thought implicit in much of what was said at the time: that George VI in some way embodied the nation, and that when he died something died also in all his subjects. Few people would have stated the case with the bluntness and clarity employed by A, but the view was widely held. Churchill apart, there was no other Briton of whom the same could have been said; and while Churchill had earned the honour George VI enjoyed it *ex officio*. It was the King, not the individual, who 'was the British people'; he might have forfeited the title by misconduct but in no way could he have earned it save through his monarchical status.

The attendance at the funeral itself was far smaller than at the Coronation some fifteen years before, nor were there the giant stands to increase the sense of occasion. The flavour of the crowd, however, was curiously similar. There was the same passionate preoccupation with any minor feature that might help to pass the time: whether a woman in the house opposite was holding a monkey, a parrot or, as it finally turned out, a Siamese cat; speculation about the ages of the other spectators. The arrival of the dustmen caused much merriment, though less ribald than at the earlier ceremony. There were no popular songs, though

'Land of my Fathers' and 'Abide With Me' were both heard at various points along the route. Only when the gun-carriage carrying the royal coffin passed did the comparison break down completely. All men took off their hats, there was absolute silence, and most people stood rigidly at attention. One Mass Observer felt 'a strange sense of guilt and irreverence' because his concentration was divided between the crowd and the procession.

As soon as the coffin had passed and the crowd began to disperse the spell snapped. The usual chatter ensued: 'I didn't see Churchill'; 'Did you see the Duke of Windsor?'; 'I saw the young Duke of Kent. He looked very pale. They say he's consumptive'; 'Did you see the Queen's wreath? Lovely, wasn't it?'; 'I'm more than pleased I came,' said a working-class woman of forty-five. 'We could have seen it on television, but it wouldn't have been the same; it's so artificial,' was the comment of a middle-class woman of fifty-five. 'This was such a colourful sight.' There was still a mood of exaltation but what had briefly been a rite of sacred significance had become a mere spectacle. 'Do tell me, how do they manage if they want to spend pennies?' asked a woman in the mid-sixties. 'I don't see how anyone can go all those hours. I've thought about that at every big event . . .'* A Mass Observer mingling with the crowd as it dispersed thought that the people were genuinely saddened by the King's death and that, though they said little about it in public, they privately felt a sense of personal loss.

Though there was ample coverage of the ceremony on television this was the last great royal occasion to be primarily an occasion for sound radio. 'It was beautiful and very moving,' said a woman of fifty-five. 'I started to cry . . .' Some factories closed for the day, in others work stopped while the broadcast was on. The streets were almost deserted.

---

* Nor was she alone in doing so. Speculation about the size of the royal bladder is one of the more common subjects of debate among the less reverent at every similar function.

A few months later old Queen Mary died. 'Well, you might as well take the plug out of your wireless,' said a plumber of forty, gloomily. 'They're at that lark again.' 'So they should when royalty dies,' retorted his wife. 'Well, if it's a reigning monarch like the last King, it's all right.' In the mood of the nation in February 1952 almost anything was likely to be all right. Though there was no shortage of cynics or dissenters the death of the King produced a wave of loyalty and affection around Britain which hardly any event in his life had equalled. The Coronation of Queen Elizabeth II was to show that the mood, though not permanent, was equally far from fleeting.

CHAPTER FIVE

Coronation, 1953

Britain in 1953 was in a mood to celebrate. The painful years of austerity that had followed the war seemed at last to be ending; the first hints of a new and undreamed of affluence were sprouting like spring flowers from the sere soil of winter. All that was needed was some strong stimulus to catalyse the growing sense of hope and confidence. The dawn of a reign provided it to perfection. Any new monarch would have done; the fact that the Queen was young and female, however, added a new dimension to the rejoicing. 'I think people are taking more interest in the Coronation because Elizabeth is a young woman,' noted a middle-aged mother from Guildford, 'and England seems to have been rather lucky with Queens in the past. We're all expecting her to work miracles, I think.'[1]

The Queen's name was as important a factor as any. Though hazy about the finer details the British people – or at least the English – associated the reign of Queen Elizabeth I with prosperity and expansion. Drake, Raleigh, the Tilbury speech, the Armada, the vast self-confidence of Knole or Hatfield, all were potent symbols in the popular imagination, signifying the birth of national greatness. The Coronation was therefore to be a rebirth; the new Elizabethans would march united into a brave new world. The Empire was already crumbling but the Commonwealth still seemed a powerful reality. Bound together by its common monarchy it would grow in strength and cohesion. Britain, still clinging valiantly to the trappings of a great power, would regain her proper place in the world. A new age, a new millennium, was dawning.

Such rapturous visions were, of course, rarely articulated with any precision. At first, indeed, the reactions most frequently heard to the forthcoming ceremony tended to be those of scepticism and mild boredom. 'Preparations and celebrations are starting much too soon,' complained a London schoolgirl. 'By the time it arrives we shall be tired of it.' As with every royal occasion the vigilant guardians of the public purse were early into the fray. 'I think it is important and necessary for international reasons,' declared a fifty-two-year-old transport inspector portentously, 'but I object to local governments spending rate-payers' money on it.' 'I want to know where all this money comes from,' speculated a fireman. 'It's my opinion they're using the War Credits on it, and that belongs to us, you know.' The *News Chronicle* spoke for orthodox left-wing opinion when it deplored the government's readiness to squander national wealth on trivia, and contrasted such extravagance with 'the cheese-paring policy towards education and welfare'.[2] All this was familiar; what was new was a shrill awareness of our poverty compared to other nations. 'It is England's Queen that is being crowned and it is the Americans that can afford to see it,' was typical of a dozen complaints about the high price of seats.

In February 1953 a national poll[3] established that only 44% of the population at that date definitely intended to participate in the Coronation, either by watching or listening to it or by joining in local festivities. 56% felt either enthusiastic or moderately approving against 20% who disapproved. By April the proportion intending to participate in one way or another had risen to 69%; a Gallup Poll showed that two million people meant to be present as the procession went by – double the figure for 1937. By May a poll in a London working-class area showed over 70% of the people either pleased or very pleased about the Coronation and less than 15% to any degree hostile.[4] These are shaky grounds on which to establish any definite trend, yet without doubt in the national debate during the first six months of 1953 the voice of criticism became steadily more muted and interest and enthusiasm grew from day to day.

The group least affected by this new euphoria was the small band of stalwart republicans. 'I don't think sodding sausages about it and that's frank . . .' said the forty-four-year-old wife of a doorman. 'It's a bleeding waste of money in my opinion. Why they've got to go through the streets like Lady Godiva beats me; after all, she's only got the same blood in her veins as you and me.' Stalwarts of this kind were not to be won over by a few newspaper articles and the promise of a party. But those who had originally been luke-warm became eager, the eager fanatical.

A survey indicated the main reasons for this approval. At the most materialistic end of the spectrum were those who rejoiced in the money that the Coronation would attract to Britain. 'Very good thing for the country – bringing foreigners to spend money here,' said the fifty-four-year-old wife of a vet. 'The bigger the show the better. It will bring lots of Americans with their dollars,' rejoiced a retired bank manager. Nor was it merely the national interest which benefited. A men's outfitters in Northampton offered ties bearing Union Jacks. 'A tie for loyal Queen's men!' read the placard. 'You are requested to purchase one of our Coronation ties as a gesture of loyalty to HM Queen Elizabeth II from the loyal citizens of Northampton.' The manager of Neon Ideas Ltd thought that his trade had been boosted by 50% at least. 'Of course, the beauty of it is, when the Coronation's over, we can remodel them and they can be used for something else.'

An argument that would certainly not have been heard in 1937 was that the monarchy was a bulwark against extremism and the Coronation therefore a blow for political stability. 'Royalty is a big expense but it helps to keep down Communism, and as long as they do that they're worth it,' summed up a forty-four-year-old bus driver. 'It's a good chance to show the unity of our Commonwealth,' felt a woman clerk of thirty-seven. The note of national self-approval, that in some way we were scoring off other nations, was perceptibly more strident than at the last Coronation. 'I'll say one thing,' said a middle-class man of sixty. 'I think the Americans are a bit jealous. They like it, they think it's wonderful and all that; but they're just a little bit jealous, as if they wished it was theirs.' 'We seem to be trying to make a come-back as a great nation,' wrote a rather more sceptical teacher from near Middlesbrough, and the feeling that the Coronation was in some way a gesture of self-assertion, a statement that Britain was reclaiming its rightful place in the comity of nations, was the explicit or implicit justification for many who would otherwise have deplored the expense and wasted effort.

The Coronation was to provide a fresh start, to wipe the slate clean after thirteen years of hardship and travail. 'With the start of a new reign a new start will also be made in politics throughout the world . . .' was the expectation of a twenty-seven-year-old housewife, while another housewife, two years older, rejoiced that years of war and austerity had been endured and we could now 'celebrate the return of better and happier living'. The lid had come off, said a retired civil servant, and we could have a fling. 'It was a psychological release of which people had latterly been deprived.'

The swelling excitement, and above all the materialism and commercial exploitation of the whole affair, did not escape criticism. 'Everybody who has anything to sell is out to sell a few more on the Coronation racket,' the Bishop of Liverpool indignantly told the Rotarians. The Vicar of Bures was still more comprehensive in his denunciation. 'The Queen can do little unless she has behind her and around her a re-dedicated nation. It is not going to help her or help the world if while she is making her solemn promises the great body of people are swilling beer and enjoying themselves in worldly pleasures.' Nor was the feeling of revulsion based always on such idealistic grounds. 'I've nothing against the Queen,' protested one shopper, 'I'm just absolutely sick of seeing her face on everything from tinned peas upwards.' 'Them moogs,' grumbled a similar critic, 'I'm fair sick o' the sight o' them. And who wants moogs, any road?'[5]

The build-up to the Coronation spawned its traditional crop of feuds and jealousies. In Barnsley the members of the Co-operative Society protested loudly because their souvenir tea caddy bore the portrait not of the Queen but of their president, Mr Herbert Wilde.[6] The parishioners of a Northumberland village appealed to their bishop because the vicar forbade the use of the church hall for a Gala Coronation Beauty Competition. But these were trivial blemishes on a mainly harmonious and massive national effort. It was naturally in London that the effort was most apparent. Sixty-eight stands requiring 4300 tons of steel tubing were erected by the Ministry of Works alone to seat its 110,000 official guests. Some 1750 standards of timber, each as high as Nelson's Column, were used in the work. Accommodation was required for 43,000 troops from overseas.

Decorations began to smother the city, above all the processional route. The Westminster City Council spent £70,000. The Regent Street Association provided 1000 waterproof and dirt-proof roses, five feet across and costing £21 17s 0d apiece. The connoisseurs scorned such excesses. 'We shall not be sorry to see the end of decorated London,' wrote John Summerson with hauteur. ' – this litter of strung bits, bearable only as the days mount to *the* moment, intolerable hereafter. Tom-toms cannot din louder than the pelmets so unrhythmically hung in some of our streets . . .'[7] But this was far from being the popular reaction. The conversation of a group of East Enders up to see the sights is far more typical:

> 'Isn't it lovely? Look, there's the Lion and Unicorn up there.'
> 'It's like a fairy tale!'
> 'It's wonderful. Makes you feel proud of London.'
> 'It's marvellous. It's a tonic.'
> 'Better to spend it on this than guns.'
> 'They've caged Eros in. That golden cage looks lovely.'

A woman of thirty-five appraised the ensemble with measured pride: 'It is like fairyland, with arches and banners across the roadway. There is no doubt about it, it is very artistic. I have been all over France and never seen anything like it. The British go all out and stop at nothing. Take America, they just drop streamers and confetti. There is nothing in that but a lot of clearing up.'

The motives behind the decorations were as mixed as their aesthetic success. The Westminster Council no doubt felt its £70,000 well spent in maintaining the pre-eminence of the borough. The Display Manager of Selfridges was delighted by the reaction of the crowds to the store's lavish decorations. 'It gave people a lump in the throat. They didn't look on it as the glamorization of a building, they realized it was a sincere tribute to the Queen.' He was asked what effect it had had on trade. 'Well, let's be honest about it. It did us a certain amount of good . . .' In Portsmouth a proper circumspection was observed: 'While it is right that Portsmouth must pay all honour to the Coronation, it has to be remembered that its decorative motifs have also to serve for the Agricultural Show on Southsea Common.'[8]

The reasons for decorating private houses were equally varied. Householders in a particularly festive part of Fulham were asked why they spent so much money on flags and banners that would serve only for a day. 'To brighten the place up; make it a bit gay', was a common response; 'To make the children happy – give them something to remember' as often advanced. Not many people made any reference to the Queen, though 'To show appreciation', 'It's the least we can do', and 'She deserves it' were among the replies recorded. Almost a quarter of those asked replied, more or less, 'I couldn't be the only person in the road without a flag'; a statistic that throws light both on the British instinct to conform and our national inability to communicate with our neighbours.

By a fortnight before the Coronation it was difficult to be in Britain, impossible to be in London, without constantly being confronted by evidence of what was about to happen. In the artistic world, for example, there were paintings of British sovereigns at the Royal Academy, Coronation pictures in a Ministry of Works exhibition in Whitehall Gardens, panoramas and models commemorating previous Coronations were on display at the Tea Centre and an exhibition called 'British Life since Elizabeth I' at the Burlington Galleries. An arts and crafts exhibition in Sutton Town Hall featured a model of Nonesuch Palace made out of match-boxes and a tea-cosy bearing the royal arms. In Finsbury Town Hall hung sixty pictures by local children on the general theme of the Coronation. Of the forty-nine by boys two featured the Queen, of the eleven by girls seven – an illustration of the repeatedly demonstrated fact that women are far more interested than men in the royal family and the personalities who compose it.

The theatres were equally obsessed. The Crazy Gang were at the Victoria Palace in 'Ring Out the Bells'. The opening words of the show were: 'Two wonderful events take place this year. The Coronation and twenty-one years of the Crazy Gang.' The show was punctuated by Coronation jokes – a member of the Gang in drag said that she'd made her knickers out of a Union Jack. She couldn't think why they were so uncomfortable. Then she found she'd left the pole in. The finale featured a musical fight between a lion and a unicorn; the Gang, in red robes and coronets, watching with approval.

The most commonly heard tune was 'In a Golden Coach', rendered with particular success by Donald Peers.

> In a golden coach
> There's a heart of gold
>   That belongs to you and me.
> And one day in June
> When the flowers are in bloom
>   That day will make history.

Noel Gay sold 200,000 copies of this inspiring lyric. Next best was 'Coronation Waltz' at 80,000 and other successful titles included 'Queen Elizabeth Waltz', 'A Waltz for the Queen', 'The Queen of Everyone's Heart', 'Britannia Rag', 'Coronation Rag' and 'Windsor Waltz'. At the Marble Arch Corner House on 30 May the band played 'Land of Hope and Glory' to loud clapping; a series of national songs of which 'My Bonnie is Over the Ocean' was best received; and 'In a Golden Coach' performed to tumultuous clapping and applause.

The provinces were slower to build up enthusiasm. The feeling that this was a London affair persisted until the very day, and even then was not entirely broken down by the chance to participate offered by the television. 'It's going to be a great affair,' said a Barnsley housewife '– that is, in London. It won't make much difference to me.' 'If I was a Londoner I'd think it was great,' commented a garage mechanic from Leeds, 'but we are too far north to be really interested.' The managing director of a company specializing in decorative material said that nearly all the interest had come from Birmingham or further south. Scotland was worst of all. 'We haven't had much from the north. I don't think they bother so much.' A pen manufacturer with a line in commemorative models confirmed that this was so, but believed, 'they'll wake up. They're just as interested really, but they don't like to make a fuss about it.'

In London enthusiasm seemed to grow in inverse ratio to the prosperity of the inhabitants. In affluent Phillimore Gardens on 30 May only a quarter of the houses were decorated; in a working-class to lower-middle-class street in Penge the figure was three-quarters. A slum street in West London, already scheduled for demolition, was garlanded from end to end with bunting and Union Jacks. Every house had pictures of the Queen and the Duke of Edinburgh in its windows. A local newsagent described the inhabitants as 'mad for royalty'. A university lecturer who canvassed regularly for the Labour Party in a working-class housing estate and also in a richer part of town noticed that in the latter the Tories usually decorated their houses, the Socialists did not. In the housing estate there was no such distinction: virtually every house was decorated.

The Queen herself was attracting ever greater attention and adulation – ranging from the Duke of Wellington who spoke of her 'astonishing radiance – her lovely teeth, hair and eyes . . . then add the wonderful voice and the romance'[9] to the private in the Dorsetshire Regiment who told a Mass Observer that the people were 'rallying round our young Queen. She's very beautiful, ain't she? There's no doubt about it at all, they're proud of 'er and are rallying around 'er.' But though her sex was for many people one of her main attractions there were those who took a more traditional line. A taxi-driver of fifty-five deplored the absence of a king: 'Well, it's the same as in any ordinary household, it's the man who's looked up to, the man is the responsible one.' In a working-class district of London 110 people were asked whether they would prefer a king to a queen. Sixteen said they would, seven preferred a queen, the vast majority were indifferent.

Total indifference was an attitude increasingly difficult to maintain. A meeting of a Labour Party General Management Committee broke up in disorder when the notoriously left-wing Party Agent admitted that he had spent 9/6*d* on decorating the headquarters. One member began to read from Keir Hardie while another shouted that, if it wasn't for the monarchy, we should be just like Russia or America. An old party war-horse boasted that he was treasurer for his local Coronation street party, upon which an equally battle-scarred veteran bellowed: 'Down with the Monarch!' 'No one seemed indifferent,' commented the Observer. 'I haven't seen my colleagues so roused for a long time.'

Converts to the Coronation spirit came apace. A retired civil servant in Morecambe professed a left-wing disdain for ritual inappropriate to his profession and residence. But: 'during the last two or three weeks I find I am getting excited by it, almost against my will. The festival spirit seems to be in the air.' A woman of fifty-nine 'felt very blasé about the Coronation almost up to the end of May . . . I got quite excited, however, a few days beforehand.' Trade in the shops bore witness to the euphoria, as well as the influx of visitors. Overall sales were up 6% on 1952, in London 12%. The take in cafés and restaurants went up by 25%, in jewellers and suppliers of fancy goods by 35%, in confectioners an astonishing 65%.

A hunger for excitement and spectacle consumed the nation. 'England has been kicked on her backside too often,' protested an RAF man outside Westminster Abbey. 'This has worked up a bit of fervour. What we want is fervour!' The eyes of the world were felt to be on London; of heaven, too, in the opinion of a lower-middle-class woman of forty-five who deplored the effect of the rain on the decorations. 'I can't understand how we can have had such weather when they are such a good family. They are so good and kind, it seems wicked to have had it all spoilt like this.' (It is fair to say that others saw divine intervention in another light, like the lady who disapproved of the display of martial might in the Coronation procession. 'I cannot feel this weather was accidental . . . God's end of it, the Abbey service, was taken care of under cover.')

Child: 'Is that it?'

Father: 'Yes, quick! Wave your flag, Maureen. Wave it high! Yes, *she's* inside it. She's *in* the coach! There it is, the top of the coach. There, you've *seen* the gold coach, Maureen.'

Mother: 'You *saw* the gold coach, Maureen, didn't you? Now, if anyone asks you, you *saw* it. Don't ever forget!'

This dialogue catches vividly the almost magical significance attached by many to seeing the Coronation in the flesh. Maureen had had no more than a glimpse of the top of a coach. She would have taken in much more on television, could have listened to the radio in comfort or studied the innumerable photographs and written accounts. But she had participated, she had *seen* the gold coach. She would never forget it. No doubt her recollection now is of an uninterrupted view of radiant beauty, a smile and wave directed personally at her. To the millions of people who crowded the Coronation route, the hundreds of thousands who spent twenty-four hours or more in damp discomfort on a pavement, the fact of participation was all important. To them the gentlemen of England now abed should properly think themselves accursed because they were not there, in Piccadilly, in the Mall, on Coronation Day.

For many, indeed, the discomfort was an essential part of the ritual, even actively enjoyable. A policeman chatting with a middle-aged man in the early hours of Coronation morning remarked that he had just been talking to an Indian in the Mall. 'He'd been there forty-eight hours. And he couldn't see. The crowds moved up on him. He's gone home. I've been on since dawn and I'll be on again from two to six.' 'But we've been here for longer than that,' replied the man. '*And* for fun. You get paid for it!'

They had been there, spread out two or three deep along the route, since noon the previous day. By 1 a.m. on 2 June, Coronation Day, a Mass Observer found Trafalgar

Square already very crowded:

> People are lying and sitting on the pavement all round
> the square, right across the pavements. They look like
> pictures of war-time refugees, or like tube shelter people;
> they form a sea of bodies, heads over-lapping on to other
> people's legs. No space at all between one body and
> another. It is raining, steadily but lightly. Some have
> formed tents on the edge of the pavement using metal
> street railings from which they have hung coats, mac-
> intoshes, newspapers, blankets. On one of these is a
> pencilled notice HOUSE TO LET – written across this,
> SOLD OUT. There is constantly a noise of an ambulance
> bell, and ambulances pass up and down every few minutes.
> This is the only traffic on the roads which anyway have
> people all over them so that a way has to be cleared every
> time for the ambulances to go through.

The analogy between the crowd and wartime refugees
occurred to another Mass Observer a little way off in the
Mall. 'It looked just what I'd imagined a refugee camp
would be like . . . everyone looked dishevelled . . . they were
sort of roaring – not really, but it sounded like it . . . They
were all rolled up in cocoons, and there were also lots of
people walking up and down – you could hardly move –
looking for places, or just watching.'

It was not only this sombre aspect which reminded people
of wartime crowds but also the good nature and friendliness
of the participants. People talked easily with total strangers;
little groups would join together in spontaneous unity;
relationships with the authorities, particularly the police,
were relaxed and tolerant. A lower-middle-class woman of
twenty-eight, mingling with the throng in Piccadilly,
remarked how wonderful it was 'to feel the old wartime
camaraderie and friendliness. The British people (and I
say this as an Irish girl) are so very restrained and reserved
as a race until there is a great national event which unites

them all . . . then I think they become the most wonderful, kindly and good-humoured people in the world.' As in 1937, there was little sign of resentment between the various classes or between seat-holders and those who sat it out in the streets. The coachman of one of the few peers to attend the Coronation in his family carriage was urging the horses to greater efforts. 'Don't be too 'ard on 'em, mister,' he was urged. 'They're only used to the milk round.' Gangs of young men wandered around jeering at the sleepers – 'Want to be tucked up, duckie?' 'Get you a hot-water bottle, darling?' – but there was little malice in their words. The front line purposefulness of the scene in Trafalgar Square was matched by spontaneous revelry only a few hundred yards away in Jermyn Street. In a pub there, the atmosphere rendered all the more convivial by the fact that it was long after the traditional closing time, someone was playing an accordion, people were singing, two women, one wearing a man's cap, were dancing a sort of lancers in the public bar. A sing-song was taken up in the saloon bar. The participants, predominantly lower middle-class, jumped up and down, keeping time, while the men slapped their legs. The most lustily rendered songs included 'When Irish Eyes are Smiling', 'How Much Is That Doggy in The Window?' and 'It's Only Because I'm A Londoner'.

By 7 a.m. on the morning of Coronation Day London was awake and bent on celebration. In the Mall the news was broadcast from loud-speakers attached to the trees. There was clapping when the announcer referred to the large crowds which had spent the night out of doors along the route; loud clapping and cheers when he said that 'some people appeared to be sleeping as soundly as if they were in their own beds'; ironical clapping at the forecast that heavy rain and cold weather were to be expected. Here as elsewhere, the news that Everest had been climbed for the first time caused a fresh bout of patriotic zeal. The news-vendors were having a field day. 'Walk up! Walk up!

Guaranteed waterproof edition,' called one man. 'Come on, Lady, you don't want just one. Got to keep both legs dry, haven't you?' 'Singing in the rain!' was another seller's slogan. 'Whose rain? Queen Elizabeth's reign, of course!'

At Marble Arch, at 7.15 a.m.:

Two sandwich men pass. Their placards say 'The Wages of Sin are Death' and 'Jesus Christ is everlasting Life'. A small group of young middle-class men watch. One says: 'This is all rather embarrassing. I mean, what are we supposed to do?' They open a suitcase, take out cards, start pontoon. Everest news is given again. Two women comment. A (a working-class woman of sixty): 'Oo, isn't that good!' B (lower middle-class of forty-five with a Lancashire accent): 'What?' A: 'The expedition's won. Wonderful, isn't it?' B: seeming uninterested, 'What weather!' A: 'Not like what we had for the Jubilee, is it? Daresay it will clear.' B takes out milk bottle with 'God Save the Queen' top on it.

News broadcast, 8 a.m. Pips get cheered. Announcer says: 'This is the Coronation Day of Her Majesty, Queen Elizabeth.' B: 'As if we didn't know,' but there are claps, cheers and some shushing. Announcer talks of those sleeping out; 'At times the temperature dropped to 44°.' A little laughter, and more when he talks about people dressed in newspaper and blankets who are sleeping soundly. Radio announces community singing – a number join in with 'Two Lovely Black Eyes', 'You Know What Sailors Are' and 'Nellie Dean'. Sun comes out and is greeted with uproar. One man pretends to salute the sun. From the radio comes, 'It ain't going to rain no mo', no mo''. Much laughter.

A Mass Observer noticed how those present all seemed to be wearing a sort of uniform. In St James's Street the men in the stands were almost all in grey, the women in duster coats with a contrasting dress and little half hats usually made of flowers and tulle – a lot of grey and white. Schoolgirls wore grey fitting coats and white gloves, their brothers navy blue blazers or grey suits. There was as little variety among the overnight squatters. The young wore duffel coats, slacks and jerseys; working-class women of thirty-five or more dark coats and head-scarves.

The service was broadcast by loud-speakers along the route: as audibility diminished away from the broadcasting points so attention faltered with it. When the Archbishop proclaimed: 'Sirs, I present unto you Queen Elizabeth, your undoubted Queen,' there were cries of 'God Save the Queen' from a group in the Mall. The noise attracted other people's attention, and, for the first time, the bulk of the crowd seemed aware of what was going on:

> Now there seem to be even fewer people walking about, more concentrated listening. The Queen's voice says 'I will'. There is practically no noise at all. 'All this I promise to do', she says. There is a little murmuring from the crowd and silence again. Observer is conscious of annoyance at the continued cries of newspaper men. The Queen goes to the altar. Still silence, perhaps a little embarrassed. A man lights a cigarette, puts it out again. The Queen takes the oath and there is anything up to a minute's complete silence. A working-class boy calls out impatiently 'Is she Queen yet?' No one answers him. Then the Communion Service. Music begins, some talking starts . . .

Inevitably concentration wavered. A group of young men from the middle class began to chatter: 'I expect the crowd will go crazy. I know I shall'; 'The pubs shut at eleven tonight'; 'Must get some hooch! Here's to Everest'; 'Just what the doctor ordered.' 'She kneels before the altar . . .' went on the commentator. 'Shush!' called a young man, and for a few moments silence fell again. It did not last for long. 'The Queen looks at Prince Charles,' said the commentator. This remark is well received by the women present.

'He's there, then!' Suddenly there is the sound of guns, accompanied by a gust of heavy rain. 'Someone's dropped an atom bomb,' says a working-class woman of sixty.

Many people saw nothing until well on into the afternoon when the procession passed their point on the return journey. Until the last minute there was the threat that the view would suddenly be snatched from them. At the corner of Regent Street and Glasshouse Street a military detachment took position as the sound of the bands grew louder. There was turmoil:

> 'Oh look, we can't see a blamed thing!'
> 'Oh, we spent the whole night here . . .'
> 'Oh, no!'
> 'Oh, look, the policeman's going to stand there as well.'
> 'Officer, we can't see a thing.'
> 'Oh, it's not fair!'
> 'Oh, crikey!'

In Trafalgar Square a Mass Observer noted the frantic efforts of those at the back of the crowd to see something of what was going on. A man clambered on top of one of Landseer's lions (he was soon turned off). 'Ah, this is cruel. Ah, that's how unlucky a man I am. When I get up here and see something, the band turns round. That's how unlucky a man I am. It's bloody sabotage.' Periscopes were in wide use but rarely gave satisfaction.

> 'I've got a nice view here.'
> 'What have you got?'
> 'Well, I *thought* it was something.'
> 'Ah, what a shame. After sleeping out two nights and that.'
> 'Now I've lost it again.'

Even when people *could* see, the problem of what they

were seeing often proved insoluble. A group of women speculated at Oxford Circus:

'They're cadets.'
'No, they're Americans.'
'They've their stripes on upside down.'
'Americans do.'
'No, they're Australians.'

And from another group a little later:

'Those are Scotties!'
'No, they're Airborne.'
'They've skirts.'
'Haven't they got funny hats?'
'Aren't they lovely?' (A conclusion which gained general assent.)

However poor the view, however miserable the weather, the passing of the procession caused a great upsurge in national pride: 'There ain't no other nation what could do nothing like this'; 'Just shows you the old bulldog breed'; 'The Yanks have nothing like this.' 'It makes you proud to be British,' said a forty-five-year-old woman with patent fervour. 'It makes you proud to be Church of England,' replied her companion with equal sincerity. The Mass Observation Archives contain several reports from those who had approached Coronation Day in a mood of scepticism or distaste, only to be converted on the road to Westminster Abbey. 'Of course, I know really that it's all a Conservative ramp,' complained a middle-aged Labour voter from Hampstead, 'but all the same there's something very moving about it, very impressive. I was astonished at the intensity of my feelings. I was annoyed – really, it's against my principles to feel like that.' 'I didn't expect to feel excited,' wrote a woman who had jeered at her husband for insisting on watching from the Embankment, 'but I was very moved by it at the end.' A twenty-one-year-old bank clerk wrote of 'a rising excitement in myself, much to my own surprise. And when the State Coach finally appeared I had eyes for nothing else.' Previously he had written to Mass Observation that he thought the Queen supercilious and remote. 'I am horrified now. The feeling is genuine, not that of one who feels he has committed sacrilege, but of one who has unwillingly noised abroad a lie.'

There were also the hard-core recalcitrants. The Local Government Officer who printed 'Down with Monarchy' across his mirror, hung up a picture of the Queen with a red arrow pointing to the waste-paper basket, and stuck pins into soap effigies of the Queen and Prince Philip, was not likely to prove susceptible to a vision in a golden coach. Yet even among such extremists one sometimes detects an uneasy regret that they were cut off from a source of national joy. 'I found the day a little depressing,' said a woman of forty-eight, 'in that such a large number of my fellow citizens appeared to be taking part in something the significance of which escaped me.'

It was television that ensured a national participation in the Coronation far more extensive than ever before dreamed of. Millions of people who could not or would not have watched the procession itself and would only have listened desultorily to a radio broadcast found themselves absorbed by the BBC film of the event. Even the most strident critics were converted, at least temporarily, like the man who 'was dragged to a TV set to watch for five minutes. He stayed all day and never a sound was heard from him. This man was an anti-monarchist and practically a Communist.' BBC audience research estimated that 56% of the adult population, 20·4 million people, were viewing and a further 32%, 11·7 million, listening to the radio. The fact that the cameras were in the Abbey, featuring in close-up the most sacred moments of the ceremony, meant that the viewer at home could feel himself involved with an immediacy denied to those who waited in the streets, even of those with a place inside. Many would, of course, argue that no film, however good, could make up for not being present in person. There is no saying who is right; what is sure, however, is that for the first time those *not* present in person were given a chance to share the sensations of those who were.

Though the numbers of those who owned or rented television sets swelled dramatically in the months before the Coronation, houses with television were still relatively few and far between. The Coronation saw the apogee of a brief-lived social phenomenon, the tele-party, in which a group of friends, relations or neighbours would group together in the house of whoever was lucky enough to possess a set. A London Mass Observer travelling by underground in the suburbs at about 9 a.m. noticed how 'every family party (and they nearly all *were* family parties) were carrying bags with food or bottles. And those with just bottles grinned at each other in an understanding sort of way. They were obviously all people going to TV parties.'

A TV party typical of all the rest took place at Finsbury Drive, Bradford. Those present were A and B, a middle-class couple; C, their son, with his American wife D of twenty-five and a baby; eighteen-year-old daughter E with unpopular boy-friend F; a friend G who reported the occasion; and various neighbours who looked in for an hour or so at a time. By 10.30 breakfast had been cleared away and the party settled down to serious viewing.

G, hostile to television until converted by the ceremony itself, was bored by the crowd *reportage* and lame bits of interviewing . . . People fidgeted around, the baby seemed surprised not to be the centre of interest but settled down on B's knee. Gradually attention settled on the screen. Everything was punctuated by the young American's, 'Oh Gee!' 'Oh Gosh!' 'Gee, but you couldn't see that in America.' During two years in England she had begun to have a great and loudly expressed admiration for England, and the Coronation ceremony just knocked her sideways.

Seeing the shot of the peeresses, somebody said, 'They're not very pretty.' Young American, enthusiastically, 'No, but look at the load of ice on them!' At the appearance of the little Prince Charles, my hostess said darkly, 'I bet they've doped him with bromide.'

At some point C went out to get coffee. Then occurred a curious interruption: it must have been during the ceremony, for everybody was irritated by it. B suddenly said he didn't like coffee, he wanted tea. A pointed out he had been having morning coffee all his life; why change now? B went out, made himself a cup of tea, brought it back and upset it in the hearth. Everyone laughed rather unsympathetically. A few days later he was asked just why he had elected to change from coffee to tea in the middle of the Coronation service. He admitted that he had been identifying himself with royalty, had been thinking of Queen Mary and of her remark that telephones were not for royalty, and it came over him in a flash that he had always hated coffee, and intended to assert his (temporarily royal) will and have the tea he had always preferred.

There were several remarks during the ceremony about Elizabeth II's family resemblance. At the moment of crowning: 'God, she's *exactly* like her father at this moment.' Sometimes: 'That's her mother's gesture.' Once or twice: 'She'll look like Queen Mary when she's older, she's not really like that Scotch bun.'

The young American grew ecstatic almost to tears. 'Oh Gosh, this is *wonderful*, this is like a fairy-tale, this is something America hasn't got.' The sense of a great national tradition seemed to silence even E for a while, though she has communist leanings . . . There was a lot of pity expressed for the faithful kerb-siders, together with some division – 'People who'll queue the night before, in weather like this, must be insane.'

But as the ceremony proceeded there was certainly a

sense of growing national pride . . . Derogatory remarks
were thrown out about America, Hollywood, Russia.
Somebody said: 'This is the last dignified thing in the
world.' The only criticisms were: that more of the Abbey
itself should have been shown, that one got slight claustro-
phobic feelings after too much of that narrow stage, and
that people felt tense at the time and tired at the end,
having been full of apprehension in case anything should
go wrong – the slightest mistake or bungling would have
seemed a bad omen.

Meanwhile, in a poor London area, television and free
ice cream for the children were provided at an Ice Cream
Parlour. Though working-class rather than middle-class the
dozen or so people present seemed to have very similar
reactions to their fellow-viewers in Bradford:

A (A woman of twenty-five): 'Look at the Queen. She's
like a plum pudding by now, they've put so many dresses
on her.'

B (Woman of forty-five): 'She's got enough sceptres and
things to keep her going.'

C (Man of thirty-five): 'They won't show us the actual
anointing; it's been forbidden.'

D (Woman of thirty-five): 'It's very moving.'

B: 'Makes you proud to be British.'

C: 'Those Yanks ain't got nothing like this.'

At this point those in the Abbey shouted 'Long live the
Queen' and this was repeated by those in the Ice Cream
Parlour.

A: 'There's Charlie with his granny.'

E (Man of fifty): 'The music is wonderful.'

C: 'It must weigh about seven pounds. It's not heavy.'

D: 'Isn't it? If you have it on your head and with all
that clothes that she's got on too?'

F (A man of forty, pointing to the Duke of Edinburgh):
'There he is!'
D: 'That's the Duke of Kent.'

After the ceremony 109 people who had watched on
television were asked to mention what had struck them as
the day's most stirring incident. Forty items were mentioned
at least once but only two were picked out more than ten
times – the moment of the crowning with eleven votes and
the news of the conquest of Everest with eighteen. It is
curious that the easy winner should have been something
wholly unconnected with the ceremony, no doubt the
unexpected nature of this contribution to the festivities
struck the imagination on a day on which all else went to
plan. As always people saw what they wanted to see, as
was shown by two letters (unpublished) to the same local
paper. 'The picture of the Queen's splendid, well-trained
horses makes one more eager to try and help those poor
horses we know are ill-treated,' wrote one lady, concerned
about the plight of Irish horses shipped to French slaughter-
houses. 'I was disgusted at the cruelty subjected to the horses
taking part by the use of short, tight reins,' wrote another
enthusiast. 'It could plainly be seen that they were suffering
great strain.'

The attraction of television ensured that the local festivities, which in 1937 might have coincided with the Coronation, now preceded or followed it. 'When are you having
your party?' one middle-aged working-class woman on a
bus asked another. 'We're having it the Saturday before the
Coronation,' was the reply. 'We're not having it the Saturday
after because people won't have the same spirit in them then,
and we're not having it on Coronation Day because people
are asking this one and that one to come and watch their
television, so there wouldn't be no one would turn up.'
The first woman's street party was to be held on Coronation
Day, but only after the television was over.

Apart from this, however, no one who had attended a

street party in 1937 would have felt at a loss in 1953. In Willesden, to take a typical London borough, there were ninety-four street parties for each of which an average £100 had been raised and to each of which 100 children came. Tea, with sandwiches, jellies and ices was provided. There were games, a distribution of sweets, a Punch and Judy or a conjuror. Coronation mugs costing between 2/6d and 5/- were given to each child. Usually there was some form of re-enactment of the Coronation with a selected child crowned and imitation orb, swords and sceptre being provided by some local handiman. 'The cynical may say that the Coronation is merely being used as an excuse for a party,' wrote the local newspaper,[10] 'but there is much more to it than that. The Coronation has deeply touched the emotions of the people. Deep emotion must find some means of expression and as there is no kind of affection more pure and disinterested than that of parents for their children . . . what simple or more direct means could be found than giving a party?'

Not a penny of official money was provided for any of these parties; in each street a handful of active and concerned people, sometimes one man or woman, made all the running, collected money, ran a raffle, persuaded neighbours to make themselves responsible for the bunting, the organization of the tea, the entertainment. As in 1937 local pride was as great a stimulus to effort as love of monarchs. An indignant letter to a Battersea paper complained that a lot of attention had been paid to a particular street 'because they have £200 in the kitty. Well, the street that I live down has £400 in the kitty . . . The street that I live down is never thought of.'

In central London the same revelry followed the ceremony as in 1937. On the whole there was much rowdiness, drunkenness and noise yet little serious mischief. It does seem, however, that the fun was slightly less good-tempered than on the previous occasion. The police who tried to pull a drunk off a lamp-post were not merely booed but had missiles, including pieces of metal thrown at them. A group of young men stood in the path of the traffic and, if a car did not stop promptly enough to satisfy them, battered it with their fists and, on one occasion at least, tried to over-turn it. But the overall impression was still one of spontaneous and genuine gaiety. At a typical pub in the Portobello Road there was much singing and dancing: 'There'll Always Be An England' and 'In a Golden Coach' both earned encores. And slowly the great crowds ebbed away. Late in the evening one Mass Observer saw a woman with four small children boarding a bus in Knightsbridge. 'The family looks very tired, dusty and dirty; the youngest child pulls at its mother's hand, the others drag their flags along the pavement. They all wear rosettes, now crumpled, and hair-ribbons, now half off. Their basket is empty except for two lemonade bottles which, although empty, have not been left behind.'

'What's happening about the Coronation here?' a Mass Observer asked a sixty-year-old man in Leeds:

'I dunno that anything's happening – not that I know of personally. That's more for Lunnon, I should say. [Pause] I've nothing against it. I suppose it will do somebody some good, put some money in some people's pockets. [Laughs] It won't do anything for me though. [Pause] I believe they're doing something up at the station, putting up lights. But it's all more for Londoners really. There won't be the same interest here.'

Until Coronation Day itself the feeling that it was mainly a London affair was widespread. Almost certainly, however, there was more going on in his neighbourhood than was apparent to the cynic from Leeds. In Morecambe Messrs Trumpell illuminated the oil jetty, then there was a cricket festival, a fancy dress party, a pageant and a newsboys' 'race and courtesy campaign' organized by the Newsagents Association. At Ripon forty characters dressed in Pickwickian style attended a luncheon at the Unicorn. There was Morris dancing in Walton Hall Park at Liverpool and submarines were open to the public at Birkenhead. St Albans searched the country for a chariot suitable for the use of Queen Boadicea – 'It must be historically correct,' said the pageant master. 'If we can't find one we shall have to use a milk-float.' In Heaton Mersey, in addition to the more orthodox tree-planting, maypole-dancing, bonfire, decorated bicycle competition and so on, there was a Mystery Lady Competition in which the first person to spot the Lady and accost her with the words 'You are Frizzy-Izzy-Wizzy, let's get busy, God Save the Queen' won 10/- and deserved every penny of it. There were setbacks, too. At Dundee they refused to give a 21-gun salute because the army was going to charge £25 for the ammunition; at Maidenhead the Coronation bonfire burnt down on 28 May. And everywhere there were street parties or village sports for the children, balls or dances for the grown-ups in the evening.

A small Northamptonshire village can stand for all the rest. Preparations had begun in October and £107 raised by subscriptions, whist-drives, raffles and so on. First came a service in a packed village church, then the Union Jack was ceremoniously hoisted over the school-house and the children given their souvenirs. In the wet and windy afternoon there was a fancy dress competition in the marquee followed by sports, at which every child won a prize. Children's tea was followed by an entertainer, during whose performance the adults ate in four shifts (cold meat, salad, ice cream, beer, cider and tea). After tea the boys from the near-by Approved School (who had also provided the church choir) gave a gymnastic display and there was then a comic cricket match, with men dressed as women and vice versa. Fireworks and a bonfire led into a dance at the school-house which lasted till the early hours of the following day.

Some seventy-two applications for ox-roasts were approved. At Idle, near Bradford, the North Eastern Gas Board piped gas into a field for the occasion. A complicated mass of cog wheels and rollers had been assembled. 'On top was a pathetic little ox which had been cooked to a frazzle and broken in two. It had large nuts and bolts through it and was held together with wire netting.' At Combe Bay, near Bath, an Indian boy refused a slice of meat indignantly; when asked why he replied: 'Because I am not a cannibal.' The Kinship Humanitarian Circle protested against 'this mentally degrading exhibition of English paganism', while a Labour MP put down a motion opposing such spectacles as 'obscene, indecent, disgusting and contrary to human dignity'.

Wherever television had spread, however, it was the viewing of the procession and ceremony, in homes or in the village hall, which became the focal point of the day. Where public events rashly competed with the hours of broadcasting they were usually scantily attended. An undergraduate who hoped to escape the Coronation by bicycling through the Sussex countryside was instead reminded of it by the deserted villages and fields. Wherever a house sported a television aerial the curtains were tightly drawn and only cheering or occasional bursts of music betrayed what was going on inside. At every function in the afternoon or evening the talk turned to what they had seen that morning: 'Wasn't the little prince sweet?'; 'I thought I would cry when the Queen took the oath'; and, again and again, 'Did you see the Queen of Tonga?'

In the next few days the Queen went on drives through the London suburbs. A Mass Observer watched as she drove up the Fulham Road. 'Cinderella will be here in a minute, won't she, Mum?' asked a girl of five. 'She always calls her that,' explained her mother. 'I can't stop it. She likes to think she's a sort of fairy girl, it's the books, what they make her look like in the picture books I suppose.' The crowd was thick; to be sure of a place near the front some people had been waiting for several hours. When the car finally

swept by there was sustained cheering and everybody waved.
A group of working-class women talked excitedly as they
dispersed:

A (aged thirty): 'Isn't she just *lovely*?'

B (aged twenty-five): 'It was worth it. I'll see her sitting
there for days.'

C (aged fifty): 'Now for a cup of tea.'

A: 'She looked so sweet, and that hat, she was sweet.'

B: 'Did you see him give a little wave too?'

'. . . not forgetting Mr Jackson, who gave
invaluable help with the fireworks.'

In Hampstead she was more than fifty minutes late. A
group of women began to speculate when the car was still
far away: 'That's her, in the white hat'; 'Got a black hat
and costume'; 'See? With the pale blue dress'; 'Look,
there. Grey with a white flower.' A man commented sardoni-

cally, 'Go on, have a good look. Has she got nylons on?' She was only in front of this particular group for a few seconds and the impression was one of breathless satisfaction.

'Saw a bit of her hat, that's all.'
   'She looked smashing.'
   'A nice little figure.'
   'She was there and gone so quickly.'
   'They both look just like their photographs.'
   'Well, do you think that was worth it?'
   'She was worried people wouldn't take to her, but she don't have to worry!'

Two impressions recur frequently in accounts of these progresses. The first, a reflection of the little girl's belief that the Queen came out of a fairy story, was surprise and gratification at the discovery that royalty was human after all. 'They're beautiful children,' remarked a woman of fifty, 'and their little actions are the same as our children's, aren't they? Just the same.' An injudicious gesture by the Duke was greeted with delighted comment: 'Oo, look, he scratched his nose! Did you see, Edith, he scratched his nose?' The other was the conviction, particularly strong among women, that the Queen had smiled and waved personally at them. Time and again the transitory vision was followed by exclamations like: 'She looked straight at me. Did you see, she looked straight at me and waved?' Whether the quality lay in the royal smile or the imagination of the spectator, some rapport was achieved as the car whisked by. Its establishment, indeed, provided the principal justification for the royal drive-arounds.

'The country and Commonwealth last Tuesday were not far from the Kingdom of Heaven,' rhapsodized the Archbishop of Canterbury a few days after the event. His words were extravagant but they reflected a mood of exaltation, a feeling that the Coronation had been more than just a royal ceremony but something involving the whole nation in a spirit of high dedication. Of course, there were many like Kingsley Martin who found such affairs no more than '. . . magnificent atheistic spectacles. They have a religious setting, but to most people they are holidays, beanos, jollifications on an immense scale.'[11] In June 1953, however, such cynics were rare, their voice almost silenced.

Some of the reasons why the Coronation of 1953 enjoyed so massive an impact have already been mentioned: the yearning for celebration after the years of austerity; the youth and good looks of the royal couple; the feeling that the ceremony symbolized the birth of a brave new world. It was above all the power of television, however, which convinced people that this was *their* Queen being crowned in *their* Cathedral, dedicating herself to *their* service. It was, of course, magnificent material for the cameras – immeasurably though techniques have improved and much though colour has added to the glory of such spectacles, the force of the old film could still be recaptured when it was shown again early in 1977. Yet it was not the pageantry and the flamboyance which struck a chord in the heart of a nation but the presence at the centre of it of a naturally shy and retiring woman, thrust by circumstances into the limelight. The film brought home, as no other rendering could have done, what the Coronation was about. The Queen's pledges to her people; her patent sincerity and dedication; the burdens that – literally as well as metaphorically – were being heaped upon her: all struck the viewers with a freshness and immediacy that had been achieved, that could have been achieved by no earlier ceremony.

'I am sure,' said the Queen in her speech that evening, 'that this, my Coronation, is not the symbol of a power and a splendour that are gone, but a declaration of our hopes for the future.' With the benefit of hindsight it is easy to be cynical about such hopes. In the immediate aftermath of the Coronation it was difficult not to share them and link them to some extent to the woman who had just been crowned. In June 1953 the Queen of England was the object of public interest and adulation more concentrated, more exclusive and above all more personal than could ever have been the lot of an earlier monarch. The nation would have joined with the sixty-year-old woman who wrote in her diary that night: 'Surely with such a Queen, we should be entering a new and better age.'

CHAPTER SIX

The Democratization of the Royal Family

In the years after 1953 Britain entered the age of the psephologist. More and more often allegedly representative cross-sections of the British people found themselves interrogated about their views on abortion, religion, washing-machines, national politics or pornographic films. On thirteen occasions between 1953 and 1976 they were asked, in various terms but with much the same purport, whether they would prefer to see the monarchical form of government continued in Britain or wished the country to become a republic. The proportion of people favouring a republic was: 1953, 9%; 1956, 10%; 1958, 14%; 1960, 10%; 1964, 16%; July 1969, 10%; October 1969, 16%; October 1970, 10%; June 1971, 19%; January 1972, 12%; May 1973, 11%; February 1976, 8%; May 1976, 10%.[1] After twenty-four years, therefore, the proportion of republicans had barely fluctuated. There were, of course, variations within the period but the most extreme of these – 16% in October 1969 and 19% in June 1971 – were accounted for by the fact that they immediately followed adverse publicity arising from greatly increased royal expenditure. The former figure was anyway contradicted in a rival poll by the *Daily Mirror* which asked a slightly different question and got an answer of 10% instead of 16%. If these two freakishly high figures are ignored it seems that 11% of the population were opposed to a monarchy throughout this period.

Though reasons differed, the attitude of this 11% was clearly defined. This was not true of the remaining 89%, who covered a spectrum from the most fervent royalist to diffident 'don't-knows' or cynics who felt the institution irrelevant to the needs of the twentieth century. The simple division into abolitionists and conservationists concealed a plethora of different points of view; still more, it cloaked a significant evolution in the way the people considered their monarchy: an evolution which was not merely spontaneous, the result of changing circumstances, but also contrived, the fruit of a more-or-less deliberate exercise in public relations by the royal family and its advisers. The twenty-five years between the Queen's accession and the Jubilee was marked by a considerable and on the whole sustained campaign to democratize the image if not the reality of royalty in Britain.

The first event of importance, however, seemed to reinforce the traditional attitudes of the royal family. In 1953 the nineteen-year-old Princess Margaret fell in love with a former royal equerry, currently Comptroller of the Queen Mother's household, Group Captain Peter Townsend. Though the fact that the Group Captain was a commoner wholly without aristocratic pretensions might have given cause for hesitation, his gallantry, good looks and excellent standing with the rest of the family would have led to his acceptance if only he had not been divorced and his wife still alive. In 1953 this seemed a crippling impediment. Townsend was packed off to Brussels for two years and the question of what would happen if the couple still wanted to marry when he returned was shelved in the hope that it would never arise.

Neither Princess Margaret nor Townsend were so obliging. In 1955 the Group Captain returned. By October the affair was maturing into one of those open secrets in which only the British public is unaware of what is being debated in the gossip columns of the world. On 24 October *The Times* broke the silence with a portentous editorial, which carefully

'*Naturally, Cleopatra, neither of us wants this little
friendship of ours to get talked about.*'

abstained from any criticism of Townsend himself but
concluded that the marriage would strike at the roots of all
that the royal family represented. Not everyone was so
generous to the Group Captain. 'Ah well, looks as if Townsend will always have to work for his own living,' jeered a
young father from Sparkbridge, while a woman teacher
commented sourly: 'All the nice young fellows she had to
pick from, and she only fancies another woman's leavings.'[2]
In the main, however, there was little criticism to be heard
of either party, though much of the match itself.

In London there was some hostility to the claims of romance. An elderly car attendant in Lowndes Square, where
Townsend was staying, described the scene. 'And the crowds,

they were black as night – hundreds and hundreds of them just standing here for hours on end, waiting to catch a look at him. Silly, I calls it. Although, mind you, he's not a bad-looking fellow.' Asked what the people were saying he summarized it: 'They say that a man of his age ought to know better. She should have lain off and known he wasn't for her.' Outside Clarence House a fifty-year-old woman from Manchester was on the spot for the third time in two days. 'I think they overdid the publicity – no dignity attached to it – and now they're trying to make a martyr of her. She should have known better!' A younger woman from Glasgow was still more emphatic. 'What I mean to say is he's a nobody, after all, just a captain. He's no blue blood in him. You couldn't have him at the head. He's just one of ourselves.' 'I don't think the affair should have been let go so far,' summed up a working-class man of forty outside Buckingham Palace. 'But you can't help feeling sorry for them . . .'[3]

Again it is worth stressing that the feelings of the London crowd – visitors included – are usually far more royalist and traditional than those of the rest of the country. The ultra-conservative view of the woman from Glasgow found little sympathy elsewhere. A survey in October 1955[4] showed that 59% of the population actively approved of the marriage, against 17% who disapproved. Of those who disapproved more than half cited as their only reason the fact that Townsend had been divorced. When the Princess finally announced that she had decided against the match the sympathy felt for her was shared with indignation at what was felt to be the stubborn inflexibility of 'the Establishment', blighting love's young dream by its insistence on outworn shibboleths. 'The typing pool at Morgan's Crucible Works is simply seething,' recorded a woman of thirty. 'They all think she ought to have married him.'

In the autumn of 1957 came another indication of the extent to which the royal family was identified by some with the stuffier forms of traditionalism. Lord Altrincham, editor of the *National and English Review*, devoted his August issue to the monarchy. In his own article on the subject he criticized the Queen for bearing the debutante stamp: 'Crawfie, the London season, the race-course, Canasta and the occasional royal tour' would not have satisfied the first Elizabeth. The second Elizabeth surrounded herself with a tweedy and socially exclusive court and spoke in public with the style of 'a priggish schoolgirl, captain of the hockey team, a prefect, and a recent candidate for Confirmation'. The article was avowedly monarchist in intent but its tone, above all the personal strictures on the Queen, raised the blood pressure of the more perfervid royalists to dangerous levels. 'I was anathematized by the Archbishop of Canterbury,' wrote Lord Altrincham ruefully, 'threatened by various backwoodsmen with shooting, horse-whipping, or hanging, drawing and quartering, slapped by an elderly member of the League of Empire Loyalists, and challenged to a duel by an Italian monarchist . . .'[5] Unkindest cut of all, the rate-payers of Altrincham solemnly disassociated themselves from their eponymous hero: 'No town has a greater sense of loyalty to the Crown than the Borough of Altrincham.'[6]

Many therefore still felt such ardent devotion to the Crown that well-intentioned if mildly offensive criticism seemed the blackest treason. It soon became clear, however, that not everyone was so intemperate. Letters to the *Daily Mirror* in the first three or four days showed a ratio of thirteen to four in favour of Lord Altrincham, by the end of the week the ratio had shifted to four to one.[7] In the *Daily Mail* only 1% supported him on 5 August, 15% on Tuesday and 45% on Wednesday. A National Opinion Poll[8] showed that 35% of the population, 40% of men, agreed entirely with Lord Altrincham, while a further 13% were undecided. Amongst the Queen's own age group (sixteen to thirty-four) 47% of those asked supported the criticisms while 55% of the whole population approved the attack, considering the royal household too exclusive and traditional. Of those who supported the existence of the monarchy many felt it was open to improvement. 'She's a bit set in her ways,' said a teacher. 'Maybe it's because of the position she's in. But I think she ought to mix more with people not in her own set.' 'She seems a bit snobbish, but it may not be her fault,' was a farmer's judgement. 'She's not allowed to meet the people she'd like to know.'[9] The old political tradition that any wrong the Queen did reflected not on her but on her advisers seemed to apply equally on a wider stage. The Queen was believed to be herself sincere and well-intentioned, but deprived of a chance to communicate with her people by the barrier interposed by stuffy, narrow-minded and excessively traditional courtiers. The royalists whom Bateman had portrayed, turning in outrage on the man who smoked before the royal toast, now seemed more absurd and anachronistic than ever.

It would be extravagant to maintain that Lord Altrincham's article and the widespread support for his point of view were more than precipitating factors in a process which was already under way, but it is from about this time that the court seemed to be making a real effort to refurbish its image if not radically reform its way of life. Informal – and well-publicized – lunch parties now took place in Buckingham Palace, in which trade unionists, headmasters and eminent footballers were imported to broaden the horizons of their monarch. The presentation of debutantes at court was ended in 1957. The bombed ruins of Buckingham Palace chapel were reconstructed to provide a gallery in which selections of the royal art treasures could be displayed. That same year, 1957, the Queen's Christmas broadcast was for the first time televised. Prince Charles was dispatched to the preparatory school of Cheam, certainly an establishment for the elite but a greater breakthrough towards a normal existence than had hitherto been granted an heir to the throne.

Then in May 1960 came the marriage of Princess Margaret to Antony Armstrong-Jones. A commoner, a professional photographer, with a name as plebeian as Jones; this was

The man who lit his cigar before the royal toast

not at all conventional material for a royal match – even though he was also an Old Etonian and step-son of an earl. The British were in a mood to welcome any wedding for someone whom they not unreasonably felt had had ill luck in her previous venture; though there were reservations about Mr Jones among the upper and upper-middle classes, Princess Margaret's choice was a popular one among the people at large. 'I'm delighted with the news that Princess Margaret is going to keep up with the Joneses,' exulted a painter's wife of thirty. 'That makes her one of us now, doesn't it?' The same feeling that she was in some way identifying herself with the rest of the nation was shown by a tobacconist, aged fifty-nine. 'She's doing the right thing. I'm glad she is marrying a commoner. He's one of us. His family have paid income tax.'[10] The crowds that lined the processional route in London were comparable to those that had cheered Princess Elizabeth on her wedding day thirteen years before; thousands slept out on the pavements to be sure of a good view the following morning.

Most striking of all among the efforts of the royal family to popularize its image was the film 'Royal Family'. For seventy-five days on 172 locations the everyday life of the Queen and her relations was followed by the cameras. Some forty-three hours of film were shot, then cut to 110 minutes. That the results were revealing could be denied by nobody; that the film only revealed what its makers wanted it to reveal is equally self-evident. 'A large-scale commercial,' the republican champion Mr William Hamilton described it. 'It is a safe bet that an anti-monarchist film editor, let loose with the same raw material, could have wrested from it a far less complimentary image.'[11]

The film was first shown by the BBC on 21 June 1969, and repeated on ITV on 29 June – on both occasions at peak viewing hours. According to the BBC Audience Research Report[12] 68% of the population saw the film on one or other occasion, a very large figure though significantly smaller than the audience for the World Cup final between England and West Germany in 1966. (Another poll put the figure at 74%,[13] but I have preferred the BBC figures as being the more authoritative.) Many more women than men watched the film – in a proportion of nearly eight to five. The proportion of those watching grew larger as the audience grew older; only just over 30% of those between fifteen and thirty against 53% of those over fifty.* The upper-middle and lower-middle classes watched in greater numbers than the working classes, 55 and 54% respectively against 42%. Regionally the differences were also marked: 49% in London and the South East; 46% in the North and South West; 43% in the Midlands; 42% in Wales, and 39% in Scotland. The fact that it is the elderly and moderately

* These and the subsequent figures are for the BBC showing alone.

prosperous woman from London or the Home Counties who cares most about royalty is too well established from other sources to need this further evidence of its correctness.

The film presented the royal family as hard-working, responsible, mutually devoted and, above all, human: there might be rather more butlers and tiaras in evidence than was the case with most of their subjects, but what they really enjoyed was a picnic in the heather or an evening in front of the telly. The royals are people just like us, was the message – or if not *just* like us, then at least not so very different – doing a difficult job to the best of their abilities and sharing the common pleasures in their time off. To those who are perpetually taken by surprise by any indication that the Queen is flesh and blood – a high proportion of the more ardent monarchists – this struck home as a most vivid revelation.

The film was remarkably successful in changing the popular view of royalty; and, what is more, in changing it in those fields in which the Queen, in particular, had previously been thought to be weak. Thus even before the film was shown 95% of the population had thought the Queen conscientious, and this figure barely changed. Only 27%, however, had thought her outspoken and this rose to 42%; 49% had thought her powerful, a figure which rose to 64%; 69% had thought her in touch with what was going on against 81% after the film was shown. Whereas before the film the younger viewers had been far more likely to think the Queen old-fashioned and irrelevant than their elders after the viewing they more or less came into line with the national average. 'The norm is for broadcasts to reinforce existingly held opinions,' concluded the Audience Research Report. 'The fact that changes *did* occur, suggests ... that some of those who chose to view the film had attitudes towards Her Majesty which ... were seen to be so "incorrect" (in the light of the information that the film provided) that a new and different image was adopted.'

In a perceptive article written shortly after the first

showing of the film[14] William Hardcastle commented on the fact that 'Royal Family' was being quickly followed by a television appearance by Prince Charles, subjecting himself to an unscripted interview. Would the next step be a similar interview with the Queen? 'I doubt it. The refurbishing of the royal image that has been going on for some time now has been managed with some skill, and skill in this field involves the judgement of when enough is enough. My guess is that "Royal Family" is the completion of a process, rather than a herald of further revelations to come.'

His argument was vividly illustrated only a few days later when Prince Charles was invested Prince of Wales at Carnarvon Castle. Here was the royal family deployed in its most formal and hierarchical array – a reminder that for all the picnics and cosy viewings of 'Dad's Army', there was still a mystery about the Crown, a religious and spiritual significance that transcended the constitutional or social sphere. A study carried out by the University of Leeds[15] led to the conclusion that the religious element of the Investiture appealed more strongly than the pop-star, and furthermore that polls taken before and after the ceremony indicated that the focusing of 'British political religiosity' on a dignified symbol of this kind reinforced the disposition to obey secular authorities. The proportion of those who believed that the British political system worked very or fairly well rose from 60·4% to 68·6%.

The idea that Prince Charles should be named Prince of Wales was overwhelmingly popular in the nation, 86% approving against a mere 6% who disapproved. In Wales in particular (though on a small statistical base) the enthusiasm was striking, with 92% in favour, 4% against.[16] Opinions were predictably more mixed on whether or not the considerable expense of the Investiture could be justified, though even here 71% felt the money well spent and only 21% that it had been wasted. Women, of course, were much more ready to approve the cost; the young more ready to denounce it.

At the end of October 1969, in the wake of all this publicity but also after a major and much publicized increase in the cost of the Royal Household, an opinion poll conducted a special survey on the position of the Queen.[17] The overall statistics were not surprising; 84% felt Britain needed a Queen, 16% that she did not. The reasons adduced for the respective points of view are of greater interest. The pomp and pageantry of royalty were praised by 40% of all those questioned while 29% felt that it was important to have someone to whom they could look up. 'We need her because I believe in our tradition,' said a psychologist from Manchester. 'You know, roast beef and Oxford and royalty.' 'You need a leader,' said a clothing machinist from the same city. 'She doesn't interfere with the running of the country but you need a Queen to look up to, don't you?' 20% believed the Queen kept Britain stable and united – 'no Queen and we'd be like France and that would be horrible' commented a shop-manager from Suffolk – while 90% felt she helped our relations with foreign countries and stimulated tourism. Among those hostile to the monarchy the most common complaint (10% of all asked) was that the institution was powerless and obsolete – 'We don't need a monarchy because it's old-fashioned, it's out of date and it's no use. It may have been some use in the past but it's nothing now.' Only 6% felt that it cost too much.

A single opinion poll is a dangerous basis on which to generalize. *How many* people approve or disapprove of the royal family can be stated with some confidence, *why* they do so is more difficult to establish. There is, however, another source of information which throws interesting light on the findings of this poll.

CHAPTER SEVEN

The Hamilton Letters

In every generation there are professional anti-monarchists. A variety of causes underlie their attitude: genuine egalitarianism and a dislike of privilege; personal grievance based on some royal snub; the wish to find some cause that will attract attention and perhaps win popularity; a complex of all these. Certainly those who have tried to use republicanism as a jumping-off ground for political advancement have been signally unsuccessful; since the days of Bradlaugh and Dilke in the middle of the nineteenth century republicanism has never enjoyed a substantial following among politicians in this country, nor has public adherence to its doctrine been anything except an impediment to gaining office.

Over the last twenty years Mr William Hamilton, Member of Parliament for West Fife, has been the voice of republicanism in Britain. He has missed no opportunity to point out what he considers to be the extravagance and anachronistic nature of the monarchy and to denounce, in terms that some consider offensive, the misdeeds of individual members of the royal family. In so doing he has done grave harm to his own career – no one can prove that he would have held any office at all, let alone high office, if he had muted his anti-monarchist opinions, yet few among those qualified to judge doubt that this would have been the case.

Over the years he has received a vast number of letters inspired by his utterances. Of those I have read a few, less than 10%, relate to the wedding of Princess Anne and another 10% or so to other episodes, but the great majority were written in January and February 1975. These months saw an application for a substantial addition to the Civil List, the publication of Mr Hamilton's book *My Queen and I*, and a series of television appearances by Mr Hamilton related to these two occurrences, in the course of which he appealed to members of the public to write in and say what they thought about the issues.

Of some 8000 letters I eliminated those written from abroad and those in which no definite attitude towards the monarchy or Mr Hamilton could be detected. That left me with a total of 6968. The first question was how many of these took the side of Mr Hamilton and how many of the monarchy. This might seem simple to establish, but in fact was not. A lady from Darlington, for instance, began her letter: 'I am with you 100%.' Here surely was a staunch supporter for Mr Hamilton; yet she continued: 'Like you I think that our dear Queen does a wonderful job and cannot be praised too highly . . .' Two letters, both from addresses in the West Country, pose a typical problem. The first correspondent clearly intended to support Mr Hamilton, criticized the extravagance of the royal yacht and the imperfections of certain members of the royal family, yet concluded that the institution of monarchy had better be preserved. The second strongly disapproved of Mr Hamilton, conceded that the royal yacht was extravagant and certain members of the royal family imperfect, but concluded that the institution of monarchy had better be preserved. The first correspondent ranked himself against the royal family, the latter for it, yet the arguments and conclusions of both correspondents were very similar. In such circumstances it has seemed best to respect so far as possible the intentions of those who wrote the letters and accept the fact that there is a grey area where people might as logically be included on one side as the other.

If we allow for this imprecision a rough breakdown shows 4043 letters for Mr Hamilton and 2925 for the royal family. This statistic tells one something about the sort of people who write to Members of Parliament, but it would be naïve to imagine that it bears any relationship to the division of opinion within the whole of Britain. The real interest of these letters lies in the composition of the correspondents within the two categories and, still more, the arguments which people advance to support their position. These letters cannot tell one how many people are for or against the monarchy, but they can give a fair idea of *why* the writers think what they do and, to a lesser extent, what sort of person supports what line of argument.

Take first the balance of sexes within the two groups. In many cases it is impossible to establish the sex of the writer, but of those who defend the monarchy and make clear their sex nearly three-quarters – 72·5% – are women. This might merely suggest that women have more time or derive greater satisfaction from writing letters to public personalities, yet when it comes to those who oppose the monarchy just over half, 51%, are men. All opinion polls show a higher proportion of royal supporters among women than men, but the disproportion is rarely recorded as dramatically as this. I had expected some regional variations, but for the most part these were not substantial. The overall pattern for and against the monarchy (42% to 58%) was slightly more pronounced in Wales and Scotland (where the anti-monarchist vote rose to 60% and 61% respectively) and less noticeable in England (where the figure was just over 57%). For England alone the variation was more striking – north of the Wash Mr Hamilton's supporters numbered 62% of total correspondents while in the south the corresponding figure was about 54%.

Of those who oppose the monarchy, the spectrum of opposition ranges from those who consider at least some reforms are necessary in the institution as it stands at present to those who would abolish the monarchy, confiscate all its property and, in a few extreme cases, execute the present incumbents. Of these 32·1% are avowed republicans, but a fair number more probably would be if they were challenged to state their position exactly. At a guess between 50 and 60% of those who wrote in support of Mr Hamilton would like to see the monarchy come to an end, either immediately or in a relatively short space of time. It is not surprising to find more declared republicans amongst the men than the women – 36·6% to 27·6%.

Nine points occur far more frequently than any others in the arguments put forward by the anti-monarchists. These are mentioned 2319 times in all, and the percentages which follow are based upon that figure.

Four times more people oppose the royal family on economic grounds than on any other – indeed, more than half the total of 2319 referred to above (51·3%, to be exact) are variants on the economic argument. The variants, however, are considerable. They overlap too much to be divisible numerically, but it is true to say that they fall into four main categories enjoying more or less equal prominence.

The first and simplest argument is that it is unfair that the Queen should have so much while others – usually the writer of the letter – have so little. Many letters consist of little more than a long recital of hardships endured by the correspondent, contrasting the lot, for instance, of a widow with three small children and a disability to that of Princess Margaret. 'I object to even One Penny of my husband's hard-earned money contributing to making the world's richest woman richer,' wrote a working-class woman from South Shields. 'Last week we had to choose between new shoes for the children and keeping up the payments on the telly. I'd like to see Prince Andrew or Prince Edward with holes in their shoes!' 'In respect of the huge pay increases being given to the royal family,' wrote a man from Glasgow, 'it would appear the Great Train Robbers were only amateurs.'

More people probably take this line than any other, but almost as many argue that the country could not afford the monarchy in the straitened circumstances of 1975. 'We can't afford a Royal Family,' claimed an old age pensioner – a

Conservative from the Isle of Cumbrae. 'It is these parasites who are sucking our life-blood and dragging us down to destruction,' wrote a more strident Londoner. From Newcastle a lady wrote: 'It most certainly proves something [exactly what she did not divulge] that countries like Japan and Germany without the monarchy are in a much better state financially than we are . . .'

The second most popular variant on this theme was that put forward by a retired miner from Gateshead: 'I don't begrudge them what they need but they ought to pay taxes like the rest of us. It's not fair that the Queen should be the richest woman in the world and not pay a penny tax on it.' 'Letting them off paying income tax makes my blood boil. Everyone else has to pay tax, why not that lot?' asked an eighty-year-old from Durham. The feeling that the Queen enjoys a fortune of vast but unknown dimensions and that it is wrong that she should not be taxed on it is widespread among these correspondents, as is also the belief that any exemption the Queen enjoys should not be extended to other members of the family. This argument is customarily put forward by the most moderate of the critics of royalty. 'Even my wife believes that they should be subject to the same taxes as we are . . .' wrote a republican doctor from Truro – the 'even' betraying a pretty sense of what he expected from a woman.

Final – and least prominent – among the economic arguments was the contention that conspicuous royal expenditure set a bad example to the country. '. . . all this unrest and strikes lies fairly and squarely at the feet of the Royal Family,' wrote a housewife (a Liberal voter) from Bournemouth. 'To have handed vast sums of money to the already fabulously wealthy family without a murmur is abominable and asking for trouble. The miners have every right to be angry . . .' The cost of Princess Anne's wedding was held to be a particular affront to the poor and the industrious: 'I just hope,' a non-political woman from Rye wrote with some bitterness, 'the pensioners found their bread and cheese a little more palatable for watching it, the homeless and jobless a little warmer and more wanted, the assembly-line operative more content with his work.'

Far more than any abstract principle it is money which is at the root of British republicanism and money which taints the otherwise total commitment of many loyalists towards their Queen. Even among those who believe that the Queen deserves her money there are many who feel that the largesse is distributed too far and that undeserving cases are living fat at the country's expense. 'I will happily support a King or Queen,' was the view of one self-styled royalist, 'but I see no sensible reason whatever why I should support an army captain, a photographer, plus, plus, plus . . .' A lady from Devon equally admired the Queen, 'who I think is a good wife and mother and a fine example to the world. But when princesses marry their husbands should support them.' Very nearly a quarter – 23% – of those who criticized the royal family without specifically professing republican views based their attitude on the proliferation of 'hangers on' around the court.

It is above all the royal princesses who are deemed to fall into this category. There are 550 hostile references by name to members of the royal family in these letters of which Princess Margaret and Princess Anne account for 323 or 58·7%. Princess Margaret comes easily first with 35·1% and Princess Anne second with 23·6%. The Queen Mother lies next with 13·8% and only then come the men; the Duke of Edinburgh with 10% and the Prince of Wales a mere 6·4%. Other members of the royal family are virtually never mentioned by name, though there are occasional derogatory references to 'lesser princelings' or 'the small fry which hangs around the court'. The most commonly voiced criticism of the Prince of Wales is that he is too perfect: 'That incredibly smug young man', a woman from Stoke described him, 'nicknamed by so many "Eric" after the *Little by Little* horror who never put a foot wrong in all his blameless life.'

'The whole set-up is ridiculous and out-of-date; the trotting horses, the plumes, the gold coach, and all the other trappings nauseate me.' The traditional pageantry associated with the monarchy, which for many people is its most attractive feature, ranks second only to economic considerations as the factor earning most disapproval. 278 people – 12% of the total – agreed with the seventeen-year-old girl from Hammer Lane whose remark is quoted above. She deduced from it that the monarch was irrelevant to the needs of the twentieth century – 'as out of date as the penny farthing bicycle', thought a Somerset man. 'Britain lives by production and exports.' A man from Glasgow – sharing the curiously prevalent illusion that if he gave his name and address his letter would be passed by the Post Office to the police and he would face victimization – made the point that 'we used to be told they held the Empire together but that is out of existence so what now?'

Those who claim that the monarchy is anachronistic usually consider that it is also relatively harmless; a slightly smaller but still substantial group – 10·8% of the total – oppose it root and branch on the grounds that they are opposed to any privilege based on birth. These – predominantly male – are the hard core of the republicans by principle. 'History shows us conclusively,' writes a man from Brixham, 'that it is an institution to maintain the dominance of the wealthy. It has been responsible for the loss of millions of lives. Its inbreeding produces people of below intelligence. It is quite undemocratic.' A lawyer from New Zealand, settled in London, commented that it was 'the ravages of the class system, the keystone of which is the monarchy, that has appalled us most about this country'.

A development of this argument was put forward by 131 people, 5·6% of the total. 'The worship of any authoritarian image, regal or political,' wrote a man from Littleborough, 'will lead to a world full of weak, sheepish, easily-led ineffectual human beings. How can a society that claims that certain people, by birth or divine right, are better than others, be a truly democratic society?' Monarchy not only represented privilege, it perpetuated it by dulling opposition and fostering a sense of deference. 'The spectacle of normal, sane people extending uncritical, near-hysterical approval to an extraordinarily privileged family clique is totally incomprehensible,' wrote a correspondent from Co-operative Street, Stafford. 'It is about as sensible as slaves supporting slavery. In fact it probably indicates a slave mentality, a relic of the days when commoners knew their place and respected their betters, and as such is a dangerous sign – these people would quite happily accept a dictatorship if they felt the right people were in charge.' A Liberal from Ilford put the same argument in a more sophisticated form: the existence of a monarch, he held, arrested people 'at a fantasy, childish level of immaturity . . . a whole society can collectively revert to childhood in its relationship with a fairy-tale mother'.

A much smaller group, only 2·7% of the total, deplores the foreign blood of the royal family. 'Who exactly are they?' asks a housewife from Humberside. 'With German blood on the one side and Greek or whatever on the other, they cannot even claim to have good English blood.' Another woman from Hull would 'prefer to have the descendants of that much maligned man Richard III – Duke of York, not the family of today'.

Only two other arguments figure frequently enough to deserve statistical enumeration. 2·2% of the total believed that the existence of the monarch divided the nation: 'How can we be united,' asked a miner's son from Yorkshire, 'when the existence of these parasites reminds us all the time that we are two nations, rich and poor, privileged and unprivileged?' Almost exactly the same number of people make the chief cause of complaint against the royal family that they patronize blood sports; it is notable that of the forty-eight people who support this line all but one of those who disclosed their sex (thirty-nine) were women.

One point that I had expected to be made frequently

yet which in fact only occurred ten times was that put forward by a man who gave no address: 'These palace lackeys should be given the deep six! A lot of snobs all from the same school no doubt. Without that tie-in they would starve.' A few other arguments are sufficiently remarkable to deserve a mention. Several people had grave doubts about the Queen's title to the throne. 'Would it be feasible to trace the Royal lineage?' asked a seventy-seven-year-old from Cornwall. 'There is a rumour that Queen Victoria had no children. If so, how come we have a Queen?' A lady from Snodland had excellent reason for knowing these doubts were justified. 'I hold documents from an Astrologer stating that there is no one greater than I and I am ordained by God to be Saviour Queen. I am also ordained by God to become the wife of Mr Heath and I have the right to ordain him King Edward I. I have had the documents since April 1972. I am now waiting for them to materialize.'

Others did not doubt the legitimacy of the royal family but adduced historical arguments against their worthiness to rule. 'When a clear-minded person thinks of the terrible murders of the wives of King Henry VIII,' wrote a republican from Abbey Wood, 'it proves the ruthfulness of the royal family.' A man from Blackpool knew that *Lady Chatterley's Lover* was based on the true facts about Queen Victoria and John Brown – 'The Tory press never publish my views,' he concluded wistfully. From the outskirts of London came a still more forceful argument: 'I should make quite clear that the Royal Family have been interfering with myself and other individuals in Richmond. I went to the police about this but got nowhere. This family is definitely following people around. I have much evidence against them . . .'

A final point of more serious interest was put forward explicitly by only eight writers but was hinted at by many more. The Queen did not use her power enough. A lady from Norfolk felt that the Queen should have taken a stronger line on the Common Market. 'I know we have a "constitutional monarch" but in the last resort, if monarchy is to have any value at all, there must be a point beyond which it will *not* go, a final sticking-point to give the crown meaning.' A male pensioner from Devon put the point still more bluntly: 'The Queen has not done anything for the people. She has to sign every law before it's lawful but never once has she said "I cannot sign this as it's detrimental to my subjects."' Distrust of politicians and hankering for some sort of authoritarian solution is far more conspicuous among the supporters of monarchy than its detractors, but it is still to be found among the latter.

Two points occur in the 2925 letters which support the monarchy far more frequently than any reasoned argument: that it is unfair to attack people who cannot answer back and that, if Mr Hamilton does not like the system here, then he should go elsewhere – Russia usually being specified as an appropriate destination. By far the largest group of letters, 683, contains nothing but abuse or threats. (Abusive language is not confined to Mr Hamilton's critics: witness the Glaswegian who wrote: 'I think you are write. The Queen is a Bastard and princess anne is like a horse and prince charles is a stuck-up toff and a poof.') These range from thirteen pages of packed invective to the brisk 'Fuck off Hamilton!' 'I'll have your balls for bacon,' threatened a housewife from Edinburgh; 'You are not unlike Hitler to look at, a real slimy rat!' contends a pensioner from Royston. A few of the letters are modestly inventive: 'You are like a load of bananas; yellow, spineless and bent.' Others are menacing: 'Four or five of us are drawing lots to decide who shall do it. Now don't go whining to the police.' To read a large number of these letters at a time is an experience unlikely to improve one's view of human nature.

Of the 1365 cases in which genuine arguments are advanced in favour of the monarchy the largest group – 298, or 21·8% – in effect ask the question 'What would be better?' It is assumed by all these correspondents that some form of head of State is necessary, and Mr Hamilton is challenged to put forward any alternative which would be as cheap, decorative and efficient as the British model. 'Look around the world, Mr Hamilton,' wrote a housewife from Exeter. 'Can you honestly say that any other country has a system which gives its people better value for their money? Would you really rather have some money-grubbing politician with all the fuss and expense of elections every few years?' 'If we ended up with a president like Nixon or Amin, well God forbid!' wrote a working-class woman from Liverpool. Nixon and Amin are the two examples regularly cited in this respect, while in such few letters as I have seen from earlier periods Nasser and Sukarno are the villains.

The implication of many of these letters is that the alternative to a constitutional monarchy is likely to be dictatorship. One hundred and seventy-four letters – 12·7% of the total – maintain specifically that the monarchy is a protection against any form of extremist government. 'It is my strong opinion,' states a lady from Letchworth, 'that should the Monarchy be removed, it would be a very short step to a Dictatorship and the Secret Police'; 'Our royalty is protection for us, the General Public,' wrote a female pensioner from SW19, 'from over-clever politicians, who given a chance would become over-powerful dictators.' Most writers clearly have in mind a dictatorship of the left, but there are those who see the Queen as the most sure protection against a right-wing military coup. A Londoner who clearly had little affection for royalty nevertheless argued that it was essential because Britain was a pagan country which needed to worship idols: 'The desire is satisfied in the young by pop-idols and footballers and in the middle-aged and old by Kings and Queens. If they are deprived of this outlet they might turn to a Hitler or Enoch Powell.' It was often maintained, as here by a clergyman from Wrexham, that the existence of the monarchy was the 'very guarantee of the democratic freedom which allows you the privilege of being their harshest critic'.

It is the glamour and human interest provided by the

royal family which provides their strongest justification to 11·9% of pro-royalists. 'There is little enough colour or imaginative display in poor old England these days,' writes a woman from Ealing, 'without you trying to get rid of the small amount we still have left.' And the pageantry had a deeper significance. 'Do we not need a colourful figurehead?' a man asks from Bath. 'Is it not part of ritual that stimulates a feeling of belonging, of being a part of something larger than yourself?' A schoolmaster from Harrogate evokes vividly the intense and personal involvement many people feel with all connected with the monarchy:

> I have followed the Royal Family since I was seven. I have collected many books and I have my own album in which I keep newspaper cuttings; these, at the time I write this letter, total 2641. My ambition is to meet the Queen and I hope one day to write a book about her. In fact my whole life revolves round royalty and were we to become a republic I would pack my bags. I follow our Royal Family religiously and have shared with them their joys and sorrows. I would give my life for the Queen.

For devotees of this calibre a glimpse of royalty is contact with the sublime. From Musselburgh another woman recalled the delight when King George VI and his family drove past her primary school more than thirty years before:

> How we pushed each other to get a better view and how proud we were that Princess Elizabeth waved back to us. I don't think even the teachers had a car between them, but none of us questioned the right of the King and Queen to be driven in one. We looked upon them as the head of the family and we loved them for passing 'our' school and letting us see them.

A more practical viewpoint is adopted by the 11·3% who

'If the Bevanites ran the Coronation . . .'
Cummings *Daily Express* 1 June 1953

believe the monarchy brings money to the country. 'Do you imagine the tourists come here to see you, Mr Hamilton?' asked a Londoner. The crowds thronging outside Buckingham Palace would not be a tenth as thick if there were no royal family ensconced inside it. True, the monarchy cost a lot to maintain, but the money all flowed back to the country and the royal family were major employers. The royal tours abroad were also believed to be great stimulators of exports: 'Trade often doubles the year after the Queen visits a country,' reported an amateur statistician from Newport.

Slightly less people, 10·7%, believed that the monarchy was a precious part of our national heritage which must on

no account be squandered. Some felt that anything which
had endured for so long must merit preservation; a lady from
SW16 enquired: 'Our Royal Family are descended from
Egbert in the year 802, so who are you to want the Monarchy
abolished?' Others were more rhetorical; from a country
house near Doncaster a lady wrote: 'The Queen is like a
lighthouse on the rock of tradition. Steadfast and firm,
standing above the stormy seas . . . Put out the light and
we founder, perhaps with all hands lost.' The contrast
between 'a semi-literate Scottish peasant' and the illustrious
monarch of 'what is still the greatest country on earth'
seemed particularly striking to a writer from East Grin-
stead. 'You are completely blind to the nobler features of

our heritage and Crown, so who are you to criticize those who are infinitely superior to you?'

Next, at 8·8%, came those who believed that 'in honouring and serving the Queen, as good citizens in peace and war, we quietly feel our patriotic love of country and unity with our like-minded fellow citizens'. The Queen was above politics and therefore the only person to whom all the country could rally. She was 'above class too in a strange way', as a correspondent from Marlow noted. In a sense this cut her off from her people, but such aloofness, wrote a shop assistant from Hurst Green, 'is absolutely necessary for the perpetuation of their position'. But it was the unity of Great Britain which the Queen fostered; not more than half a dozen people suggested that, as Head of the Commonwealth, she held that body together.

Yet she was, believed 8·8%, the envy of other races. 'I can think of no single person on this globe who is more generally respected than our Queen,' declared a Lancastrian lady. Americans and Germans alike were jealous of our royal family and would dearly love a similar institution themselves. The massive television coverage given to Princess Anne's wedding by foreign countries was particularly gratifying to a female old age pensioner from Walthamstow. '. . . we were so proud that we could put it on the television screens of the world. No other country has anything to compare with this.'

Slightly less again, 7·9%, believed that the monarchy was above all valuable for the good example it set the nation. '. . . a superb example of the strictest fidelity to a great trust', wrote a man from Cheshire. 'If all other workers were as true to their contracts as the Queen, this realm would be a far better and more prosperous place.' Conscientiousness and industry are the virtues which the Queen is most often held to exemplify. 'Courage, good behaviour, good manners, decent dress and high cultural standards' was the catalogue offered from a smart address near Wolverhampton, 'the standard that makes the Englishman that much different and that much better than any other race'. As a group it was above all for the fine example of family life that they set the rest of us that the royal family was praised; 'an example that only the Holy Family can better' was the somewhat bizarre analogy of a man writing from an hotel in St Helens. Though there was one half-joking reference to a 'godly, righteous and sober life', the Queen's role as Head of the Church had hardly a mention, and her regular church-going was passed over by all but four correspondents. A few took the argument a stage further and argued that humanity had to have someone to look up to and emulate and that the Queen filled the role supremely well. 'All right-minded people must have a star to look up to, without it we will surely die,' was how it was put by a man from Perthshire.

Last of the arguments which was mentioned with some frequency – eighty-two times, or 6% – was that put forward by an old age pensioner: 'Remember all ships need a rudder to stabilize. Our Royal Family gives us this.' This is perhaps no more than a variant on the theme that the monarchy is a buffer against extremism, but the belief that royalty produces calm, good order and security is sufficiently pronounced to deserve mention on its own. 'Look around you, Willie,' urged another pensioner from Sidmouth, 'at the peace that reigns in our beloved country, then look at all the countries that have dispensed with the Monarchy. Nothing but killings and intrigues.'

No other single argument got anything approaching even 1% of the total mentions. One point surprisingly not mentioned more often was that expressed by a miner's wife at Durham: 'The Queen gives moral support to all her subjects, like a mother to her children.' Perhaps the Queen is still too young to figure as a mother-figure, or perhaps the need for so conventional a support has withered, along with the family, the Church and other such traditional institutions. It will be easier to tell in twenty years when the Queen has achieved that longevity so much esteemed in British society.

Can one draw any firm conclusions from these letters? There is none which conflicts with the consensus of other material. Women are more apt to be partisans of the monarchy than men. Money is the most important single element in the minds of those who oppose its existence. The monarch is respected above all as a symbol of stability and the source of glamour in a dingy world. But the impression which one gains most forcefully from the Hamilton letters is the extent to which people are preoccupied by thoughts of the royal family. Obviously nobody would take the trouble to write to an MP if they did not have strong interest in the subject, but these letters reveal that thousands of otherwise apparently sane and well-balanced people feel so passionately on the subject that they consider any point of view but their own as at the best absurd, at the worst vicious or treasonable. For them at least the passing of time has not robbed the monarchy of any of its savour.

CHAPTER EIGHT

The Forgotten Family?

Is not the king's name twenty thousand names?
Arm, Arm, my name. A puny subject strikes
At thy great glory.

Mr Hamilton, perhaps, might be dismissed by ardent
royalists as a puny subject, but the more subtle erosion of
indifference is harder to contend with. What was the Queen's
name worth as the last few years before the Silver Jubilee
slipped unhappily away? Did any of the 'great glory'
survive? The world-wide empire over which she was supposed to preside had crumbled almost to nothing, Britain
itself tottered from crisis to crisis. By a few the royal family
was detested; by more, but still a few, it was adored; it
seemed at times as if from the greater part of the people an
amused but apathetic tolerance was the best that could be
expected.

'Too much publicity will stain the mystery, even the
dignity of the Crown. Too little publicity will be regarded
as undemocratic and will render the gulf that yawns between
the sovereign and the ordinary subject an unfortunate
barrier rather than a necessity of segregation.'[1] Harold
Nicolson put his finger firmly on the problem that must
perplex any royal or, indeed, ruling family: to court publicity
and thus cheapen the currency or to avoid it and risk un-
popularity. Every fresh step that the Queen takes in the
direction of democratization will probably be acclaimed by
the great majority of her subjects; yet at the end of the day

may monarch and subject alike find that they have destroyed the institution that they set out to improve?

Certainly the feeling that the whole business of the monarchy ought to be simplified, streamlined, adjusted to the needs of the times, is prevalent among many who support its existence. 'The State Opening of Parliament may be a splendid tourist spectacle,' wrote an angry business man to his newspaper, 'but if it can't be planned better it ought to be scrapped. The traffic in London on Wednesday was murder. My normal trip takes 10–15 minutes. On Wednesday it took an hour and forty minutes!'[2] Similar arguments based on practical considerations could be and have been adduced for abolishing almost every ritual or traditional activity with which the royal family is associated.

In 1966 a poll showed that almost two-thirds of those asked felt that 'the royal family should live more like ordinary people'.[3] 'Nowadays royalty are different,' said a machine operator's wife with satisfaction. 'They're one of us. Not like the old kings and queens who kept themselves to themselves.' They are different, in short, because they are no longer different. 'They're out and about nowadays mixing with all sorts of people,' said a forty-year-old sales representative. 'The Queen in particular does quite a lot and she's bringing up the children that way. She lets them mix with other children – they're not indoctrinated with snobbishness.' By behaving in this way the Queen was being 'modern' and 'progressive'. 'There is a change to a more modern outlook,' said a local government officer with satisfaction. 'I think they are looked on as ordinary people now.'

To be modern is one thing, to be fashionable another. Even in the mid-1960s, when progress was still in vogue, there were those who doubted the wisdom of a royal family swimming too vigorously with the tide. 'The monarchy here is different from other countries,' said a pattern designer of thirty. 'I wouldn't want it to be like it is in Scandinavia where you might hop on to a bus and who knows but you might be sitting next to a member of the royal family. I believe in being democratic but I wouldn't like that.' A property dealer's wife of fifty-six did not in the least want the royal family to be ordinary people, citing in some disgust the pattern set by the Dutch, 'riding their bicycles all over the place. Our royalty don't want to give that sort of impression.' Probably a large majority of the people at any time over the last twenty-five years would have disagreed with her; that was just the sort of impression they felt our royalty ought to want to give. But whether, when the transformation was complete and the royals had become ordinary people, there would still be any point in maintaining their royal status was a factor that did not seem to have been much considered. It occurred though to the socialist teacher from Southall. 'It's all very well,' he wrote, 'to talk about the Queen behaving more like the rest of us, but it wouldn't work. You can't have her opening Parliament in a state coach and fancy dress one day and standing in a queue at the supermarket the next. She may be just like us really but she mustn't ever admit it if she's to survive.'[4]

On one point at least there was little doubt that 'progress' was felt desirable. In 1965 near 90% of those polled thought royalty should be able to marry commoners. By 1969 the figure had risen to 93%; 31% actually favoured a commoner as a bride for Prince Charles, 62% felt that it would not matter.[5] Even of those who stood out for tradition only a handful felt that marriage with a commoner should automatically debar him from succession to the throne. A garage attendant of forty-eight must have found few who would agree with him when he pronounced balefully: 'They should stick to their own. You can't cross a racehorse with a donkey.'

However strenuous the efforts of the royal family or their public relations officers to blur the distinction between racehorses and donkeys there is little evidence that the working class has been taken in. In 1967 Frank Parkin remarked that the monarchy embodied 'values which are in close accord with the ideology of Conservatism and which, conversely, are out of harmony with the value system of Socialism'.[6] A 1968 poll in Glasgow showed that 70% of those asked took it for granted that the Queen would vote Conservative if the choice were given her, only 4% thought she might vote Labour.[7] It did not follow from this that they opposed the idea of the monarchy, even though a majority of them must themselves have been Labour voters; merely that they made a realistic assessment of the royal family's position in society. Britain was divided into 'them' and 'us', and the Queen was *ex officio* captain of the 'them' team.

Richard Hoggart in his seminal *The Uses of Literacy*[8] concluded indeed that the working class took very little interest in the monarchy. If the men thought about it at all it was with a vague hostility 'since it tends to suggest to them the world of special parades in the Services, of "blanco and bullshit" '. For a younger generation, spared the rigours of military service and with a different set of social assumptions, this acrimony must have dwindled but perhaps at the price of even greater loss of contact; the two worlds do not connect. It is hard to believe that the marriage of Princess Anne to a rich army officer or the dispatch of the royal children to an expensive private school will do much to kindle a sense of community among working-class young men of the North or Midlands. Hoggart felt that women took greater interest in members of the royal family as individuals – in the soap-opera side of royalty – but resented more keenly their riches and privileges: 'they are well cared for; they have no money troubles like us; they don't have to struggle with the kids when they are tired out; they're waited on hand and foot.' In a period of soaring inflation and wage restraint, in which the royal family are evidently insulated from the material problems of everyday life, this resentment can only be felt more sharply.

The attitude of the working class was not influenced by the belief that the royal family was in any way directly responsible for the troubles that beset them. A series of polls taken between January 1963 and November 1975,[9] designed to show where the people felt real power lay in the country, indicated that the proportion which believed the royal family held great influence was 19% at the start of the period and 17% at the end, with only minor fluctuations in between. The comparable figures for the Unions were 57% and 85%. Power, therefore, had shifted but the position of the Crown had barely changed. More than 80% thought that they enjoyed little or no power; but impotence does not necessarily earn contempt. Richard Hoggart believes, if anything, it won them sympathy: 'It's a rotten job, they get pushed around as much as we do.'[10]

Nor did indifference – if indifference there was – mean that there was also ignorance. On the contrary, all the evidence there is suggests that the people at large know far more about their monarch than they do about their politicians. In the Glaswegian survey referred to above[11] 83% of those asked could name three or more of the royal children, but only 56% could name their party leaders. 91% remembered who had been on the throne when they had been a child, against 76% who knew their parents' political allegiance. In a national poll of school children between the ages of ten and fourteen 94% could name the Queen, only 56% the Prime Minister.

Inevitably the almost obsessive interest which the public had taken in the monarchy at the time of the Coronation dwindled in the succeeding years. In 1957 30% of the population had a picture of some royal personage displayed in their houses; three years later the proportion had dropped to 20%.[12] In January 1971 a poll showed the Queen to be easily the woman most admired in Britain, well ahead of Barbara Castle and Lilian Board, with 'my wife' a poor fourth. She retained the position in December 1971, though strongly challenged by Mrs Gandhi. At the time of the oil crisis she was temporarily displaced by Mrs Golda Meir, but won back her position the following year, only to succumb to Mrs Thatcher in November 1975. (Another nugget of wisdom to be gleaned from this series of polls is that twice as many husbands list their wives as their most admired woman as wives perform the same courtesy for their husbands in the converse role.)

In an entertaining series of essays which he edited, Jeremy Murray-Brown described a royal tour in 1969 which he followed through various southern towns.[13] Each visit consisted of an 'unremitting series of handshakes, addresses, visits and presentations . . . A bewildering succession of Sussex folk bowed and curtsied to her – mayors and mayoresses, aldermen, sheriffs, chief-constables, schoolmistresses, clerks to the local councils, magistrates, deans, vicars, vicars' wardens, managers of building works, hotel keepers who could not very well be avoided as they were providing the lunch, college students and school prefects, the odd Lord and Lady who could not very easily be excluded, and a man officially described as a "representative fisherman" who presented the Queen with a basketful of Rye bloaters.' The crowd along the route cheered dutifully, which pleased the Duke of Norfolk, the Lord Lieutenant – 'I was proud of my Sussex people today' – but in the end a faint malaise seemed to hang over the participants: 'it had all been too rushed, the Queen had met too limited a selection of people . . . there had been no real communication with the people who had turned out to cheer.' A schoolboy was asked how he had reacted to the royal presence:

'I blinked and missed her going past.'
'Was it worth it?'
'Well, she means more to me than Harold Wilson does, anyway!'

Modified rapture even on the prosperous south coast, heartland of royalist fervour. In their study of the monarchy Professors Rose and Kavanagh[14] found little evidence of antagonism, still less of out-and-out republicanism, but were struck above all by what they called 'the shallowness of the British response to the Queen'. The royal family, it seemed, was as inevitable as the weather but far less worthy of discussion. Nobody much wanted it abolished, any more than there was a serious movement for the demolition of Buckingham Palace, yet who, given a vacant site, would today think of erecting Buckingham Palace to fill the gap? 'You've got to have somebody at the head,' said an Englishwoman who happened to be in Glasgow at the time of the poll. 'It might as well be her.'

It would indeed be astonishing if the public response to royalty in the late 1960s and the 1970s had been as enthusiastic as at the time of the Coronation. Inevitably the excitement generated by the dawn of a brave new world turned sour when the same old economic crises and labour disputes racked the nation, when the Commonwealth disintegrated, when Britain slipped inexorably from the first to the second and finally almost to the third league of global powers. Nobody pretended that it was the Queen's fault, but equally nobody felt that the monarchy could escape untarnished from the process of national degradation.

Even though the country had prospered, however, the first fine careless rapture of the Coronation would in time have given place to a more realistic, more mundane relationship. The link between monarch and people, as in a marriage, starts with a honeymoon but then usually passes through testing years before it matures into the total solidity of a successful relationship for life. The Duke of Edinburgh, with characteristic common sense, identified the problem in a television interview in March 1968:[15]

The monarchy is part of the fabric of the country. And, as the fabric alters, so the monarchy and its people's relations to it alters. In 1953 the situation in this country was totally different. And not only *that* – we were a great deal younger. And I think young people, a young Queen and young family, are infinitely more newsworthy and amusing. You know, we're getting on for middle age, and I dare say, when we're really ancient, there might be a

bit more reverence again. I don't know, but I would
have thought we were entering probably the least interesting period of the kind of glamorous existence . . .
I think people have got more accustomed to us. There
used to be much more interest.

Antiquated puppets stiffly enacting their prescribed
rituals against a backcloth of increasing tattiness, long after
the audience had left the theatre. The role of royalty might
have been summarized thus in 1970, and there would have
been some truth in the description. Yet it would have been
very far from the whole truth. The magical glow of royalty
survived, dimmed perhaps by the passage of events but far
from extinguished. Some time in the early 1970s Brian
Masters at a dinner party admitted that from time to time
he had a dream about the Queen.[16] 'To my amazement
everyone else at the table had dreamed about the Royal
Family as well.' He asked another thousand people or so
whether they had similar dreams; two to three hundred
not only had them but had remembered them in detail.
Nor was it only the royalist who was so favoured; many of
those who experienced such dreams had little enthusiasm
for the institution. 'It is a measure of the affection which
binds the English people to their monarch,' wrote Mr
Masters, 'that she should have entered so deeply into their
sub-conscious that even convinced republicans and militant
communists grudgingly admit that, in their dreams, she is
pleasant and charming.' A psychiatrist might provide a
different interpretation but few would deny that a queen who
sprang so readily into her subjects' dreams played a larger
part in their minds than the external evidence might
suggest. Whether one likes it or not the fact of monarchy is
engraved into the consciousness of every Briton: it can be
rejected or acclaimed, but it can not easily be sloughed
off as an unwanted and irrelevant relic.

Nowhere is this latent force made more apparent than on
those occasions when someone is exposed to direct contact

with the Queen or another member of the royal family. A woman of forty-five, lower-middle-class, described a close brush with the Queen Mother: 'She went right past us and it was as if she was looking right straight at you. You went cold right down here' (putting her hand to her heart).[17] A youth attending a party at St James's Palace: 'I could barely stand the excitement of it all and every now and then had to pinch myself to make sure that I had not dreamed it all. When I think of it now it gives me a wonderful feeling.'[18] An officer from the Fire Brigade being presented with the BEM: 'I thought it would just be another ceremony, but now that I've been, it's something I'll remember for the rest of my days.'[19] An Australian in a Sussex pub talking of the Duke of Edinburgh: 'Melbourne, it was, the week before I came home, and it was bloody great, it was marvellous. Well I'll tell you, he actually spoke to a friend of my mother's. Well, she was a neighbour, and she was in the crowd, and Philip spoke to her, this neighbour of mother's, and it was, well, I'll tell you, it was ... wooo!' He flailed his arms about in the air, unable to find words.[20]

Such incidents could be multiplied a hundredfold. Nor are they confined to the unsophisticated. An eminent man-of-letters in the early fifties, with a modicum of aristocratic blood and a temperament of detached radicalism, was invited to one of the Queen's informal lunches. He accepted in a spirit of mingled curiosity and ribaldry. The mood survived until the Queen appeared and her guests were presented. 'Suddenly I felt physically ill,' he said. 'My legs felt weak, my head swam and my mind went totally blank. "So you're writing about such-and-such, Mr – " said the Queen. I had no idea what I was writing about, or even if I was writing a book at all. All I could think of to say was, "What a pretty brooch you're wearing, ma'am." So far as I can recall she was not wearing a brooch at all. Presumably she was used to such imbecility; anyway, she paid no attention to my babbling and in a minute or two I found that I was talking sense again.' Looking back, he says that he feels not so much shame as surprise. 'I have never felt like that before. I hope that I never do again. I would not have believed that I could have reacted in such a way.'

Would this man have reacted in the same way if confronted by Marlene Dietrich, Jacqueline Kennedy, Dame Rebecca West? No, because he had met all three of them, and though he had found the first and third in their separate ways impressive he was in no way overawed. Royalty touched some atavistic chord of whose existence he had previously been unaware, a susceptibility which had survived a lifetime during which he had believed the monarchy to be a relatively harmless anachronism; something to be resented in youth and tolerated in middle age. Whether his attitude was a vestigial relic of the deference observed by his ancestors towards the Crown or whether it represented some still less rational appreciation of the mystic force of royalty was something he could not decide himself. All he was certain of was that he felt an unease, even a fear, wholly inappropriate to the circumstances of luncheon with a middle-aged lady whose conversation was certainly less scintillating than his own.

'Is not the king's name twenty thousand names?' Does the divinity still hedge a king? That the monarchy in 1976 was far less emotive a concept than it had been a quarter of a century before seemed patently evident. That some of the old magic still clung to it was equally plain. How much of it had fled and whether the loss of it was permanent were questions which the Silver Jubilee of 1977 was to help answer.

CHAPTER NINE

Jubilee, 1977

Before the end of 1976 only a handful of people had taken in the fact that there was to be a Jubilee the following year. Most of those were in one way or another connected with its organization. Among them there was a mood of some apprehension.

There seemed good reason to fear that the Jubilee might prove at worst a fiasco, at best a pale success. Any jubilee is to some extent an artificial celebration. There is no magic in twenty-five years, no sudden novelty about those whose anniversary is being commemorated. Compared with the Coronation of 1953 the Silver Jubilee seemed likely to be an anti-climax. One would have felt this even if the intervening quarter-century had been a period of unbroken triumph. As it was, Britain had stumbled from disaster to disaster, the Queen presiding over a sustained national decline which can hardly have had its equal in any age. The Jubilee was certain to coincide with a period of stark economic crisis. Everyone knew that it was not the Queen's fault, but there still did not seem to be much to rejoice at. Her lustre would have grown from national triumph; inevitably it waned when all went ill. 'People don't seem to be taking much notice of the Jubilee,' commented a working-class woman of eighty. 'It's a shame for the Queen but I think people hold it against her for giving away the colonies for there was gold in some of them countries.'

At least the eighty-year-old had some idea what was being commemorated. Ignorance, or at best confusion, was more frequent. A housewife of forty-five from Bath, asked whether she knew about the Jubilee, replied firmly: 'This is something I could write a book about.' There was a long pause, presumably while she sketched out the opening chapter in her mind, then she continued lamely: 'I don't mind royalty: I don't mind at all.' A working-class man of sixty from the same city was still more at a loss: 'Yes, I've heard of the Jubilee. It's on 13 June. It commemorates D-Day.' A boy of fourteen was suspicious. 'Does that mean that Prince Charles is illegit?' he asked. 'I read he was twenty-seven and the Jubilee is twenty-five years, isn't it?' A belief that the Jubilee commemorated twenty-five years of royal marriage was surprisingly prevalent and still to be found almost to the day of the ceremony itself.

After 7 February total ignorance was more difficult to maintain. The decision to celebrate the Jubilee on 7 June rather than on the true anniversary of the accession meant that a false peak of public excitement was reached on the earlier date. For a few days the newspapers were filled with material about the Queen's reign; the film of the Coronation was shown again on television to a massive audience. Many people felt that, even if the Jubilee were not yet over, it ought to be. A fear of being bored was a common reaction. 'We're going to be sick and tired of all this Jubilee stuff by the time it's over,' said a woman of thirty-five apprehensively. Apathy seemed to be the mood most often encountered by those who set out to get things moving. Even in loyal Bournemouth a church worker complained: 'One simply can't get anyone to help in planning celebrations for the Jubilee. It's as though the heavy cost of living had weighed people down till they were losing heart.' In Bingley, *The Guardian* bemoaned, 'Apathy hits plans for Jubilee'.[1] A mere handful of people had turned up at British Legion meetings to discuss the programme for the great day. In Glasgow a girl of eighteen, hearing that the Queen was to visit the city, remarked: 'I don't know if I'll go and see her. Maybe if Charles were coming. He's quite nice. Mind you,

'My more spirited subjects used to globetrot while *I* stayed at home. What are all *your* Sir Walter Raleighs doing?'

he's losing his hair.'

A fear that the Jubilee would involve inordinate expense, whether national or personal, was commonly voiced – not surprisingly, given the parlous state of the economy. Councils were wasting money that should be spent on schools or hospitals; old age pensioners were suffering while elaborate plans were being laid for fireworks and processions. 'Oh, I love the Royalties, I do,' declared a farmer's wife in a small Wiltshire village. 'But this village, it's stupid. They've gone and ordered a great lot of mugs, and who's to pay for them? Us in the WI [the Women's Institute] have got to find it as usual. The Vicar! He needs grinding up afresh, that one.' But though people felt that any sort of expensive rejoicing would be out of place there was little overt hostility to the monarchy. A local feminist group at Lewes debated earnestly whether or not to participate and concluded that they should not, but this was mainly because of the sexist bias which they felt the rituals would enshrine. Such out-and-out opposition as there was had its root – as usual – in economic or material rather than philosophical considerations. The old West Country roadman who declared, 'none of them haven't never done nothing for I, and I cain't see myself doing much for they', spoke for a sizeable part of the community.

There were many who saw in the Jubilee a chance to help themselves or the country. A middle-class woman of fifty from Argyll justified the proceedings on the grounds that: 'We'll be able to make a pile of rubbish and sell it to foreigners.' There was much speculation about the number of tourists who would visit the country and the amount of currency they would bring with them. 'All the traditions of England will come out during Jubilee week . . . it will give a face-lift to a very dull England' – the sentiment was voiced by a lady clog-dancer who, in February, already had a booking for a street party in Birmingham and foresaw many more to come. To some it proved a source of cheap publicity. In Dewsbury the eponymous chairman of G. W. Mallinson Ltd thought too little patriotic spirit was being shown by the other local firms and invested in a new Union Jack. 'Three rousing cheers for Mr G. W. Mallinson, who has the courage to be proud of his Queen and country,' wrote the editor of the *Dewsbury Reporter*.

Even at this early stage real enthusiasm was already being shown. The village of Shilton, in Oxfordshire, held a torchlight procession on 5 February in the cold and pouring rain. Some sixty villagers gathered at the church beneath two flaming crosses, sang an anthem, listened to accession prayers, and then formed a circle round the village pond to sing 'Land of Hope and Glory'. 'Then the procession strag-

gled uphill; torches swinging above dark figures and reflected light streaming down the road in a wash of rainwater.
As the procession turned left past the Baptist Church torches
were spluttering out and all hurried back to the village hall
for soup, hot dogs and coffee.' Such events, however, were
the exception; in the main the ardent royalists were laying
their plans but keeping their powder dry.

'Oh, I'm sure it will all turn out very well. As soon as
people start organizing and getting together these things
always do work out well.' In February many would have
thought this seventy-year-old from Bridport over-sanguine,
but there were enough people who enjoyed organizing to
ensure that things began to move. Though they were still
often finding it hard to whip up much enthusiasm activists all
over Britain began to find out what had happened at the
last Silver Jubilee and at the Coronation, to set up committees, to consider methods of fund-raising. 'Certainly we
should mark the occasion,' proclaimed a retired headmis-
tress from a Sussex village. 'I hope the Vicar will arrange
something. I have ordered some new rope for the flagpole.
I shall hoist the flag and keep it flying.' By the end of March
it was possible to detect a mood, not so much of enthusiasm
as something close to resignation; an acceptance that the
Jubilee was going to come and that people might as well
make the best of it. A left-wing art-master admitted grum-
pily: 'It's growing from something that was small and insignificant into something that is actually going to affect
my life.'

As the country began to emerge from a singularly bleak
winter the feeling grew that it was time for a party. At this
stage the link between monarchy and celebration sometimes
seemed tenuous. 'Ain't thought much about it. Expect 'twill
be a right old booze up,' said a Bridport fisherman approvingly. A man of thirty from Derby was taking part in a
cricket match 'to celebrate, but it's only an excuse'. Favourite
projects – the planting of trees, a seat for the village green,

an annexe to the school hall – were revived and latched on behind the Jubilee bandwagon. 'All the grandeur that once was Vienna,' was to be re-created in the school at Shippey. The Further Education Tutor had had the project in mind for years: 'The Jubilee has simply given me the excuse to get things organized.'[2]

The delights of fund-raising involved many in the day-to-day preparations. To raise money for street parties in Cleveland a paraplegic in a wheel-chair challenged all comers at table-tennis; seven girls roller-skated four miles; a wandering minstrel played a guitar all the way from Middlesbrough town hall to Redcar. On Maundy Thursday 200 men and boys with bats and baldrics set off to dance their way in relays from London to Norwich. This marathon, organized by the Morris Clubs of London, echoed the feat of William Kempin in 1599.[3] In Salisbury, though a Mass Observer found 'little interest' in February, fund-raising activities were in full swing by March – a netball match between men and women, a pancake race. All over England and Wales bazaars, raffles and jumble-sales were reported.

In Scotland activity was at a noticeably lower level. 'I don't think the Scots are royalists,' said a thirty-eight-year-old woman from Inverness. There were no volunteers from the Western Isles Council to attend a garden party at Holyrood Palace. The Reverend Roderick McLeod said he would be in Edinburgh at the time and 'would accept it as a punishment if you wish me to attend'.[4] A thirty-year-old Glaswegian remarked that emotional involvement in royalty was only strong in London. 'In Scotland it seems to be confined mainly to middle-aged to elderly middle-class men and women of a conservative persuasion who feel themselves under attack and see the sovereign as a personification of their threatened standards.'

Between March and the end of May the build-up was inexorable. It could be measured in the shop windows along a stretch of High Street, Kensington, including one large department store (Barker's), a Smith's, a Woolworth's, two banks, a tobacconist's, a dozen or so clothing shops and miscellaneous boutiques, hamburger joints, travel agencies, and so on. From thirty such concerns there was a total of 109 windows (thirty-seven belonging to Barker's). In February, the anniversary of the accession, only four shops and six windows carried material relating to the Jubilee. T. Elliott's, purveyor of women's shoes, boasted a 'Celebration Offer', but 'haven't got a clue, sorry' was the response of the assistant asked of what the celebration was in aid. By the end of March the total, both of shops and windows, had dropped by one. In early May things were looking up. Barker's devoted nine windows almost exclusively to Jubilee goods, and featured a vast lion and unicorn above the main entrance. Just over half the thirty concerns in some way showed themselves conscious of what was going on, and one of the minority was anyway preoccupied by closing down. Finally, on the eve of Jubilee Day itself, only seven of the thirty were void of decoration, and these included American hamburger joints and ice-cream parlours which could be excused a failure in British patriotism. Some of the decorations were rudimentary – a tatty string of bunting or a single photograph – but several of the smaller shops had clearly devoted much time, thought and expense to their appearance. Of Barker's thirty-seven windows only two had no traces of the Jubilee. In the window devoted to china one was urged to 'Set a Jubilee Dinner Table all in Gold'; furniture bore the message, 'Traditional Leather fits into a very Royal Occasion'; while red, white and blue socks, with '1952–77' woven into the design, bore the device 'Legs Warm to the Jubilee'.

It was indeed the ingenuity with which commercial enterprises contrived to make capital out of the Jubilee which inspired the greatest wonder. Skinner's Departmental Store in Sutton, Surrey, heralded the great event with a banner reading:

Oh to be in England
Now that Spring is here,
Oh to be in Skinner's (China and Glass)
In Jubilee Year.

Anyone buying a new house from Barratt Developments
of Luton got a 'beautiful Royal Staffordshire Jubilee loving-
cup' thrown in for good measure. Mogil Motors of Oban
offered eleven used cars for sale as 'Jubilee Bargains'. An advertisement for Hoover products in the Bingley *Guardian* contrived to use the word 'Jubilee' twenty-seven times.

Much of the business generated was more directly linked
to the monarchy. Souvenirs ranged from a silver bowl
produced by Mappin and Webb at £2500 to a ½p-sticker
to be attached to an envelope or postcard. Within this gamut
were such rarities as a solid glass coach with eight horses
in a bottle – a limited edition of twenty-five at £750 each;
replicas of Coronation chairs on sale at £90; Queen Elizabeth Climbing Roses, with a 'beautiful stainless steel disc'
as a bonus; Union Jack underpants and bowler hats; more
than 600 varieties of mugs. The affluent and energetic
souvenir hunter could have accumulated, at a conservative
estimate, some 30,000 different artifacts related to the Jubilee.

Publishers were not slow in profiting from the royalist
fever. First in the field and triumphant winner in the end
was Robert Lacey's *Majesty*, an entertaining and brilliantly
contrived exercise in the art of making bricks with a limited
quantity of straw. This biography of Queen Elizabeth II
had little to add in terms of hard facts to the information
already available to the public, but Mr Lacey managed to
convince his readers that he was indeed writing from the
inside. His rich confection was vastly and deservedly successful, selling 200,000 copies by the end of Jubilee year. By
the time that book was published Buckingham Palace knew
of thirty-one others to come in the course of the year in
some way related to the Jubilee – ranging from the orthodox
coffee table picture book through the literate and intelligent

pages of Philip Howard's *British Monarchy* to bizarre accumu-
lations of postcards with a royal theme. Almost all did
respectably, some did dramatically well. On the whole it
was the unabashedly romantic picture books: Patrick
Montague-Smith's *Country Life Book of the Royal Silver Jubilee*,
or Reginald Davis's *Elizabeth Our Queen* which carried away
the more glittering prizes: the public did not want constitutional history so much as gossip and pretty photographs.

This plethora of Jubilee material generated a counter-
attack. Banners and graffiti reading 'Stuff the Jubilee' or
'Sod the Jubilee' began to appear, usually in the vicinity
of universities. In the lavatory attached to the library of
the Honourable Society of the Middle Temple this latter
device was further refined: 'Sod the Jubilee. The Ersatz Or-
gasm of the Silent Majority.' Such slogans rarely lasted for
long. Visually they were swamped by the sea of flags and
bunting which now began to emerge. Its incidence varied
from area to area. Decorations were most lavish in the poorer
areas of the cities of southern England, notably London;
generally they grew thinner as the milieu became more
conspicuously middle-class or the area more distant from
the capital. Villages differed vastly: according not so
much to the patriotism or the prosperity of the inhabitants
as the energy of the local Jubilee Committee. On a typical
council-estate in Herts seven out of seventeen households
polled in February had been apathetic or opposed to the
Jubilee. On 4 June all seventeen houses were decorated and
the seven malcontents were among the more lavishly adorned.
By the end of May there can have been few towns or
villages, few streets even, which did not bear some indication
of approaching celebrations.

The gradual waning of doubts about the Jubilee was
shown by polls conducted for Mass Observation by the
British Market Research Bureau at the beginning of February
and at the end of May 1977. At the earlier date the surprisingly high figure of 16·4% answered 'No' to the question
'Does Britain need a Queen?' By the end of May the figure

had dropped to a more usual 13·5%. As was to be expected, the number of republican males significantly exceeded that of females: 19% to 13·4% in the first poll; 17·2% to 10·2% in the second. 38·4% of those polled felt at the earlier date that the Jubilee was 'rather a waste of money'; at the later date this had dropped to 31·2%. Unfortunately figures do not exist to show the state of opinion directly after the Jubilee. It would be astonishing if the number of republicans had not shown a further decline, but it equally seems unlikely that it would have dropped far below the 11% or so which has been the normal lower level over the previous fifteen years. What one might call the professional republicans remained true to their convictions; it was the great mass of uncommitted opinion or unenthusiastic royalists in the middle that rallied exuberantly to the occasion in the final weeks before the Jubilee.

The exuberance of the royalist rally was indeed so marked that not even the most determined anti-monarchist could deny it. All over Britain a frenzy of last-minute preparation was in progress as communities which, through disapproval or inattention, had neglected to provide any form of local celebration, belatedly decided that something must be done after all. A woman who ran the museum in a small town in Sussex and had reported almost total apathy in February now wrote: 'I found the difference in the thoughts of people quite astonishing . . . Those who had said previously that they would take no part in the celebrations but would work in their gardens *were* found working in their gardens, but they had all entered for the best kept garden competition. Those who had said they would go away were feverishly preparing for the sports, carrying wood to the bonfire; building a platform for the dancing.' A worker in a Dorset fish shop looked benevolently on the hectic activity. 'Can't see us doing anything like this caper for old Jim or Harold,' he observed.

On 3 June 1977 the *New Statesman*, in an issue dedicated

largely to the Silver Jubilee, published extracts from a number of essays written by children from a London school. The tone of most of these was emphatically anti-monarchical. In this they were unlike the four London schools, two comprehensive, one primary and one private, whose pupils wrote essays for Mass Observation. The explanation for this no doubt lies in part in the predilections of the teacher; in every case it is almost possible to hear his voice saying 'one of the things you might consider . . .' or 'you may want to mention' – innocent suggestions enough, but inevitably influencing the pupils' comments.

Not surprisingly, the private school was the most patriotic. Of the twenty-three boys who wrote essays twenty-two were staunch monarchists – 'otherwise we would have fights and people would vote for Queens and Kings and some people might think it unfair'; 'they stand up for country and are very good nice people'; 'It keeps up British tradition and it is fun'; 'they help the country out of sticky positions' and, more originally, 'Someone has to own the pigeons and swans.' Only one rebel questioned the relevance of the institution: 'She hardly does any work and she gets lots of money just for bathing in the sun on holiday or sitting on the throne with a crown on her head.'

The two comprehensives were also overwhelmingly in favour, for much the same reasons as in the case of the private school. It was, however, more often suggested that the cost of the monarch was too great. 'Of course they all look very nice when wearing their expensive clothes and jewellery, but is it all necessary?'; 'I sometimes think that the money could be put to the use of curing a disease.' The rigours of the Queen's life earned her some sympathy – 'she has to shake hands till her hands drop off'; 'she spends a lot of time travelling from country to country eating loads of greasy foreign food.' 'I like the Queen very much but I prefer her husband,' contributed one twelve-year-old girl. The voice of republicanism was rarely heard but at least once was expressed most trenchantly: 'To me the Queen is nothing and she will always be nothing, because to me she's just a made-up story and I don't like it.'

It was the eight- and nine-year-olds of the primary school who most closely approached the *New Statesman* contributors. Even here only one child was unequivocally republican, and she had an American mother: 'She must be out of her mind to show herself to people like a monument . . . I would rather have a president.' A note of egalitarian disapproval, however, figured in several pieces: 'They order people around and get everything they like . . .'; 'She shows off too much and doesn't need so many castles . . .'; 'she wears too many clothes and has a posh accent'. The day after the Jubilee the children were asked whether they had seen the procession and walk-about on television. All had. They were then asked what they had thought of it. Even the American girl – doubtful, perhaps, about her safety – agreed that the Queen had seemed 'nice' and 'kind', and that the people there had clearly loved her very much.

So Jubilee Day itself arrived. The heart of the celebrations was the procession to St Paul's on the morning of 7 June, followed by a Thanksgiving Service and a luncheon at the Guildhall. It was the Coronation in miniature, but till within a few days it seemed that the contrast with the Coronation would be more striking than the similarity. There were no stands along the route, decorations were modest and largely confined to the Mall and Trafalgar Square. The Golden Coach was to be exhumed for the occasion, but only a few members of the royal family would accompany the Queen on her drive to St Paul's; there would be only a handful of troops from overseas to supplement the anyway modest British contingent; no foreign potentates, no Queen of Tonga – vast, benign and coffee-coloured – would lend exotic glamour to the proceedings. The procession, in short, was being done on the cheap, and it was anyone's guess whether it would attract crowds remotely comparable to those drawn to the great royal occasions of the past.

By 11 p.m. on 6 June the answer was beginning to emerge. The Mall was already lined with people settling into deck chairs and sleeping bags. It was evidently assumed that thieves would not be at work on such a night since possessions were left casually scattered on the pavement. There were no reports of this confidence being abused. The road itself was solid with cars, moving sluggishly in both directions. A van packed with Boy Scouts waving flags and cheering got counter-cheers from the squatters and the passers-by. Only one drunk was in evidence, but some at least of the general bonhomie may have been owed to alcohol. A group of eight or nine teenagers wearing comic hats and carrying large Union Jacks marched up the middle of the road. A girl with her head stuck out of the sunshine roof of a car busily filmed them. A group surrounded the car, cheering and laughing, and posed for photographs. Eventually they let it proceed on its way while the occupants of a police car alongside watched benignly. Less than 10% of the cars carried any sort of flag; most of them looked as if the owners had just returned from the week-end and had made a detour through the West End to see what was going on. Outside Clarence House a dozen teenage girls sang 'God Save The Queen', then:

> Two, four, six, eight
> Who do we appreciate?
> LIZZIE!

A dire old man watched the jubilation gloomily: 'It'll be different in the morning. There'll be tears in the morning.' If there were, they were quickly dried. By 9 a.m. the following morning people were five–six deep the whole way along the route and more were pouring in from every direction. At least half of them wore Jubilee brooches, carried flags or were in some way dressed to mark the occasion. Four youths wore jeans rolled up to the knees to reveal Union Jack socks bound round with red, white and blue ribbon. Another man of thirty or so wore a wig of paper flowers; his face was smeared with red and his trousers were made of green satin embellished by milk-bottle tops. Extravagance of this kind tended to be ignored by the British but was greeted with some enthusiasm by foreign tourists who presumably accepted it as an interesting manifestation of local folklore.

Of an arbitrary 2000 people advancing on the processional route approximately 6–7% were coloured. A higher proportion of these seemed to be elderly or children than was true of the whites, while there were significantly less coloured teenagers and young men and women. Those who were there however were as enthusiastic as anyone else – a young West Indian mother who appeared to have lost her daughter alternated screeches of 'Elsa' with radiant smiles in the direction of the balcony of Buckingham Palace and cries of 'Oh, no!' On the whole they seemed to feel themselves at home: 'Lot of foreigners here,' observed one Asian to another at the sight of a group of very evident Americans. It was harder to judge the proportion of foreigners to British. In front of Buckingham Palace it seemed particularly high, as much as 50% in some parts of the crowd, but elsewhere along the route it was far smaller. The attitude of the British towards their visitors was generally one of slightly patronizing welcome – here at least was something which we could still do better than the rest of the world. The greater the wonder and the ignorance of the guests, the greater the benevolence of the hosts.

'That harp's Ireland, but what's that dragon?' asked a middle-aged American peering at some royal standard.

'That's not a dragon,' replied his wife. 'It's a lion.'
'It's England, then. Where's St George?'
'What's that long thin animal?'

'That must be Scotland.'

'Poor old Wales!'

'Perhaps the harp is Wales. After all, Ireland's a republic, isn't it?'

The British caught each other's eyes and smiled knowingly, but were noticeably unwilling or unable to elucidate the mysteries.

Some people had predicted that the crowd would resemble the congregation at a typical Church of England matins: old ladies and a few representatives of the middle classes dragging along reluctant children. Reality was different. Though plenty of the spectators could reminisce about the Coronation of 1953 the predominance of youth was very evident; in a sample of 1000 people, 70% bore all the signs of being under the age of thirty. Banners or badges reading 'Liz rules, OK!' or, 'Cool Rule Liz' showed some contemporary flavour, yet the songs could hardly have been more traditional. 'Land of Hope and Glory', 'Rule Britannia', 'John Brown's Body', 'Ten Green Bottles', 'There'll Always be an England', 'It's a Long Way to Tipperary' were the tunes most often heard. A pop tune had been written for the occasion which included the lines:

> Everybody's mad about ya
> Where would Britain be without ya?
> Sailing in the yacht Britannia
> Nowhere in the world would ban ya.
> Queenie Baby, I'm not foolin,
> Only you could do the ruling,
> In your own sweet royal way.

So far as the crowd were concerned it might never have been written. 'She'll be Coming Round the Mountain when she Comes' was another favourite. 'If she ever does come,' observed a man glumly. By ten o'clock or so, however, things at last were happening. No one who had been present in 1937 or 1953 would have found reason for surprise at the reactions of the crowd. The dustcarts received the usual rapturous plaudits, there was the same anxious speculation about the identity of people who were patently unknown to any of the spectators:

'Who's this lot then?'
'Blimey, that one looks a bit rickety!'
'That one looks as if he was falling asleep.'
'Expect they're all Lord Mayors and things.'

The first full-blooded excitement, however, came with the passage of the Queen Mother and Prince Andrew and Edward. A group of teenage girls rhapsodized:

'Oh look, the cavalry, dozens of them.'
'Yeah, much more than for the others.'
'Oh, here she is!'
'Oh, she's coming.'
'Oh, isn't she lovely!'
'Oh, look, James and Andrew.'
'They're lovely boys.'
'Oh, James is gorgeous, isn't he?'
'It's all lovely, lovely!'
'We can't see. Oh! I saw her! I jumped and saw her!'
'Oh, it's beautiful.'

Inevitably it was the Golden Coach which caused the greatest stir. 'It's unbelievable'; 'It's *fan-tas-tic*!' From a seemingly prosaic man of fifty: 'It's not real, it can't be, it's magical.' Yet perhaps because of their seclusion behind the windows the crowd did not seem able to establish with the Queen and the Duke of Edinburgh the personal link for which it craved. It was Prince Charles, riding on a horse directly behind the coach, who filled the gap. 'He looked right at me! Did you see that, man? He did. He looked right at me!' A group of working-class men and women were exactly opposite the Prince of Wales when the procession temporarily halted:

'Hey, they've stopped.'
'Good old Charlie.'
'Look over here, Charlie.'
'Hey, Charles!'
'Come on, give us a smile!'
'Charlie, come on, over here!'
'You're doing well, son.'

Whether in response to the calls or by coincidence the Prince seemed to turn and nod slightly towards the group. The nod from the Commendatore's statue in the graveyard could hardly have caused a greater sensation. Direct contact had been established. The Prince of Wales and the crowd had suddenly been transformed into 'Charles and Me'.

In front of St Paul's there were many who had been there all night, while anyone with any sort of a view had been standing there for six or seven hours. There was no resentment, however, of the well-dressed guests who arrived at the Cathedral door, indeed one working-class woman of thirty-odd was positively indignant when they were made to wait outside for a time: 'They're only just letting the guests in. That's a bit bad.' Identifying the VIPs proved a welcome diversion. 'There's Harold Wilson,' called a girl of twenty. 'No, it's not, it's Macmillan,' corrected her boy-friend. Macmillan was cheered up the steps with a chorus of 'Rule Britannia'. 'Where's Mrs Thatcher?' asked the girl. 'She'll arrive in the Golden Coach instead of the Queen, you'll see!' Jokes suggesting that Mrs Thatcher was better suited to be Queen than Prime Minister, or that Idi Amin was likely to arrive in the next carriage, were often heard. Mr Callaghan was greeted with cheers but also with sporadic boos, one of the few signs of ill temper on an otherwise halcyon day.

After the service came the innovation of the day, the walk

from St Paul's to the Guildhall. The police sealed off the streets along which the Queen was to pass a long time before she began, so as to keep down the pressure of the crowds. As a result it was an intimate occasion, unsensational to anyone not standing at or near the front, admirably suited to be shown on television. A Mass Observer managed to get close to the action:

A lady in the crowd who got just a smile from the Queen smiles radiantly and makes a great fuss with her neighbours.

An Asian man, aged about thirty, to whom she speaks, stands staring into space when she has passed, oblivious to the fuss and cackle from his relations. He calmly puts a cigarette in his mouth and draws long and deep. Coming back to reality he looks embarrassed, moved, proud.

When the Queen has passed I managed to get across the road. The Asian has gone but his wife is still there. She says her husband has gone for a drink to calm himself. I ask her what the Queen said to him. 'It's nice to speak to the Queen,' she replies. 'She asked us how long we'd waited and we told her we had been here since 8 o'clock this morning. Then she asked us where we came from and we said "Lewisham".' Whispering, the woman added: 'We come from Uganda originally, we were thrown out five years ago, but we didn't like to tell her that, so we said we came from Lewisham.'

Other exchanges were hardly more stimulating. 'Are these all yours?' she asked a Jamaican mother surrounded by a bevy of children. 'No, just two of them. The rest are nephews.' 'Oh, that's all right then.' A child had just asked her father whether she was going to see the *real* Queen. Her father passed on the information. 'Now she can see I'm real,' said the Queen. But what was said was as unimportant as the platitudes mouthed at weddings or funerals – it was the contact that mattered. Sometimes, real feeling broke into the exchanges. 'We have come here because we love you,' said an office girl in her early twenties. 'I can feel it, and it means so much to me,' replied the Queen.

If she did not then she proved herself a consummate actress. The vision that came over on television was of a normally shy and restrained woman whose defences had been broken down by the discovery that she was not merely respected but loved. As she walked through the crowds, their hands stretched out to her as if she were a medieval monarch whose touch could cure, she found it difficult not to show her delight.

It was to be almost 4 o'clock before the Queen was back in the Palace but a large part of the crowd had stayed where it was and was reinforced nearer the time by many new arrivals. Sometimes it was possible to detect a feeling that enough was enough:

'Hurry up, Garry, or you won't see the Queen,' called a woman of thirty.

'I've seen the Queen.'

'Well, you're bloody well going to see her again,' concluded Garry's harassed father.

Generally, however, the crowd was as good-tempered and enthusiastic as ever. In the Mall excitement was whipped up by two jolly fellows, one on either side, who periodically issued ritual challenges to each other:

'Our side can shout louder than yours.'
'Oh no, it can't!'
'Oh yes, it can!'
'Oh no, it can't!'
'Oh yes, it can!'

And so on until boredom or exhaustion supervened. Two young men debated the size of the crowd:

'It's one million at least.'

'One million! It's two million at least.'
'Last time it was five million.'

Soon a large part of it was surging down the Mall towards the Palace. Every report stresses that in spite of the pressure and jostling, the frustration at the slow progress and the massive bulk of the Victoria Memorial blocking the view of the Palace balcony, even in spite of a sudden downpour, the people were almost invariably good-tempered and polite. The park attendants noted with amazement that the flower beds in front of the Palace were hardly trampled on by the massive crowd. The Queen Mother was spotted looking out of a window. A middle-class man of thirty called out:

'Oh, look, there's the Queen Mother watching *us*.'
'Wish she was on the balcony,' commented an elderly man.
'Oh, she couldn't do that. She's retired.'

Five minutes later she was out on the balcony with the rest of the family. Every new appearance was greeted with rapturous cheers. A female civil servant of about forty lingered on in front of the Palace:

I just couldn't bear to go away, in case she came out again – I love them all so much, you see. Then an African woman came along with her children, and we all thought they had come too late. She was going away but I said wait, you'll never forgive yourself (they were from Brixton, I think). They started to get tired and then, just as they were going home, because they were all squabbling, she came out again. And the *look* on those kids' faces, you never could believe it, they'll remember those few minutes when they're buried in their graves. And what I want to say is, does she know the effect she has? Does she know how she can win people around? I know I just love her, but I'm not biased. If she can win African children's hearts like that, she could rule the country properly, don't you think? And I want to make sure she knows that, so she can . . .

For most people the London celebrations were watched on television. Of eighteen schoolgirls in Frant, seventeen devoted more than two hours to watching the procession, service and walk-about – the eighteenth was away from home. (It is perhaps fair to note that thirteen watched *My Fair Lady* the same evening.) The scenes at Buckingham Palace moved a four-year-old child almost to hysteria. 'Mummy, come and see! It's the *Queen.* She's in *pink* with things all over her hat and her *hat* is *pink* too! Look at the people. They've got *Union Jacks*! And the Queen's up on a *window-sill*! And she's *waving* to them!' A forty-year-old sceptic from Scotland was amazed by the 'fantastic enthusiasm' of the crowd. 'So much for my earlier thoughts about waning popularity of the monarch. The media have a lot to answer for, making everyone believe that the current notions of a few are shared by all.'

It was the local celebrations which gave the nation at large a chance to express its feelings. Fittleworth, in Sussex, is representative of thousands of other small towns and villages. Events were spread over six days and included:

A Children's Day, with Carnival Floats, Fancy Dress Parade, Sports, Tea and Bonfire;
A Jubilee Supper, followed by draw of Jubilee Raffle and Musical Entertainment;
Edwardian Riverside Picnic Party with Entertainment by the Graffham Rushes;
Garden Party;
Bingo Evening;
Barn Dance;

Barbecue;

Day of Sport with Football Tournament, Cricket Match, Pram Races and Tug-of-War;

Mummers' Play;

Grand Whist Drive;

Lowering the Flag Ceremony;

Thanksgiving Service: 'The Midnight Sun', a Methodist Pop Group, will Play and Sing.

The ingenuity of the local inhabitants in devising individual features seemed endless. At Watton and Stone the usual bill-of-fare was enriched by 'piano-smashing'; in Westcott there were slippery-pole pillow fights and 'welly-wanging'. 'Welly-throwing' and 'welly-hoying' were other variants on the second theme; newly minted traditional sports involving that staple of British country life – the wellington boot. In Biggar an exhibition of royal souvenirs was held in the Masonic Hall. 'Various local people were going round literally hundreds of little exhibits while a rather wheezing gramophone played "God Save the Queen", "Land of Hope and Glory" and "Zadok the Priest". It was ingenuous, old fashioned and quite delightful.' *Private Eye*'s presentation of the plans of the Neasden Borough Council, with a tableau representing the Opening of the Original Cohen Launderama in 1952, a Display of Deepfreeze Tele-Snacks in Finefare Road and a Parade of Buses, was hardly more bizarre than some of the real happenings.

In the larger towns and cities it was the street parties which were the focal point of the Jubilee celebrations. In London there were more than 6000, in Exeter 139. Traditionally these had been confined to the poorer areas, yet in 1977 – perhaps a symptom of the erosion of class differences under the weight of television, improved public education and the levelling of incomes – the phenomenon spread to the richer streets. In bourgeois Kensington elderly bankers put on funny hats, Tory MPs manned the discotheque. In Campden

Hill a woman of forty-five remarked: 'It was quite amazing. You found yourself talking to the most unlikely people and we ended up after midnight drinking brandy in the house of someone we'd never met before.' Typical of such 'most unlikely people' was an electrician at a working-class street party in Worcester. A long-haired student accosted him with exclamations such as, 'This is great, man, great. The real community spirit!' 'I made my noises about working-class culture,' recorded the electrician, 'and he seemed suitably impressed, saying "Great, man, great!"'

A street party in the South of England, though in a middle- to lower-middle-class street, was typical of all of them in the logistic and human problems which had to be solved. Work started at the end of March. All householders had to agree to the street being closed, and the wives were duly canvassed. 'One said her husband always played snooker on Mondays and would be annoyed if he couldn't get home in his car' – she was eventually persuaded that this obstacle was not insuperable. Another agreed grudgingly to join but insisted that 'she and her husband will sit at their own picnic table in their own front garden, not at tables in the street'.

By the end of April, after several meetings and as many quarrels, 'excitement seems to be increasing. A wants to have madrigals and morris dances. One of the workers said her daughter would play the guitar and sing, another wanted to play the trombone . . . at this rate we will never get everything in.' The usual discussion took place as to whether to admit people from neighbouring streets – the decision was at first for exclusivity, but later this was relaxed. Groups were set up to organize the drink, the food, the tables, the sports for the children – 'Everything seemed to be going well when B erupted into the room and told us we were talking too much and not being sufficiently well organized.' A barn dance was decided on, which meant £12 had to be found – a coffee morning and two donations provided the answer. 'Man at the local shop is going to provide free ice cones for the kids. Amazing, he is usually rather mean.' A programme was prepared, then had to be hurriedly revised because a music committee had been set up and had ruled out the retired maths teacher who wanted to play the piano. A man agreed to be Master of Ceremonies but caused some concern by refusing to propose a loyal toast to the Queen. By the end of May £45 had been collected for the various expenses.

Decorations now became the main scene of activity. 'I bought two Union Jack plastic bags from Woolworth's, 12p each and cut them up and stuck them along the top of the garage. Hung the red Xmas streamers from the porch plus a red, white and blue flower. C drew a picture of the Queen about four feet high and stuck it on the back door.' By 6 June almost every house had decorations. One had a washing line on which all the washing was red, white and blue. A retired army officer 'wanted to put out a flag but only had a French one but he said "perhaps my wife could put a few tucks in it or something".'

The party took place on 6 June. 'The people helping me with the games wore jeans rolled up, stripey socks, red white and blue T-shirts, rosettes, flowers etc. and looked very jolly.' The games went well except for the dressing up race, which was disastrous because the clothes were smaller than the children. A group of amateur entertainers then took over. 'They dressed up in tail coats, false moustaches, pith helmets etc. and sang "Knees up Mother Brown" and "Up the Jubilee".' The biggest success was the barn dance in which almost everyone joined. A teenage pop group was followed by community singing and a torchlight procession to the town bonfire. Everyone sang the national anthem and so to bed. 'Even if none of us were too keen on the Queen,' concluded the Mass Observer, 'she did give us an excuse to have some fun. I really feel it has drawn the neighbourhood together right across the generations and probably no other occasion could have accomplished it.'

Not every occasion went so smoothly. There are accounts

'Damn Joneses – he's wearing a WHITE tie!'

of a handful of drenched spectators around a feeble bonfire,
failing to sing the national anthem with anything approaching gusto; of dances in village halls where few turned up
and the party spirit was notably lacking; of streets in which
quarrels between the organizers meant that two, or in one
case even three groups held rival parties and ill feeling was
rampant. The proud boast of the dreadful child from
Scarborough – 'before we could eat we had to sing "God
Save Our Gracious Queen". But I never sung it! After we'd
eaten, the parents put records on for us to dance. But we
never danced to them!' – was heard elsewhere as well. But
it was a rarity. More common were complaints of vandalism
and pilfering. Decorations were torn down and portraits
of the Queen defaced – whether as an anti-monarchist
protest or for the hell of it must remain an open question.
The Chairman of the Judo and Youth Club at Weston Rhyn
wrote in indignation:

The Committee and myself are proud to be British,
and for that reason flags were displayed on the Assembly
Rooms for the Jubilee celebrations. The person or persons
who tore down and stole the large Union Jack flag . . .
are a disgrace to the Country and our Community.
Do they realize such disgusting behaviour reflects directly
against HM the Queen (God Bless Her)?

Again and again, where local celebrations are concerned,
the talk is of the spirit of community which was generated,
and which could have been inspired by no other force. 'Now
we all know each other,' wrote a Mass Observer from the
Wirrall. 'The slight dissensions that arose during the long
period of planning have been forgotten in the satisfaction
of a successful enterprise. There are no strangers in the
Avenue and the children smile when they pass the adults.'
In Blackburn the community relations officer reported with
pleasure on the way in which the Asian population had
joined in and had been accepted by their neighbours[5]
(though in other reports from areas with a large immigrant
population it was remarked that the Asians remained largely
aloof). In Fazakerly, Liverpool, six weeks after the party:
'people speak together who last Christmas would not have
looked sideways at anyone. Young mothers are allowing their
children to speak and play with one another – even of different religious backgrounds.'

Six weeks is not very long. 'I bet people won't be so
neighbourly when it's all over,' was a baleful comment at
Gravesend. 'They'll go back to what they were.' The Coronation of 1953 had created a similar sense of unity; the shock
of surprise experienced in 1977 showed that the effects had
long been forgotten. Yet while it lasted it had been potent
and genuine, and it did not seem unduly optimistic to hope
that something at least would linger on. Even if it did not
people still felt it had been worth while. At Nutfield, Surrey,
there was already dissension by 1 July about the disposal of

the money left over from the celebrations. The spirit of unity seemed in peril. Yet, 'for one ten-day period we forgot inflation, local problems, personal problems, and all joined in some harmless fun – all ages, all classes, both sexes were at one. It can't be bad.'

Wherever she went on her provincial tours of England, and to a lesser degree Wales, the Queen was rapturously received. Again and again there are references to people who proclaimed that they would not cross the street to watch her yet, when the day came, crossed the city or even the county to do so. Only in Scotland was the pattern noticeably different, and even here it differed strikingly from place to place. In Glasgow, where there had been fears of a chilly reception, the success was tumultuous. A Mass Observer spoke of 'a dramatic build-up of interest just before her arrival . . . a definite feeling of fiesta'. On the day of the procession the city centre was packed, the other streets deserted. 'I loved it,' wrote a woman of thirty-four. 'I went to see her more for the kids' sake, just for a peep, but I stayed out six hours. The atmosphere in the streets was terrific.' A middle-class woman of thirty had in February recorded that she thought the monarchy was obsolete. Now: 'I was really quite surprised at the mammoth reception HM received. I even have to admit being caught up in a moment of nostalgia . . .'

In Edinburgh the reception was noticeably more luke-warm. Crowds were thin and an American couple found they could get a place in the front only a few minutes before the Queen passed. No doubt this was partly because monarchy was nothing new for Edinburgh, but a consciousness of the devolution issue seemed more marked than in the sister city. 'Who'll be the first to blow up an E II R pillarbox?' asked an Edinburgh business man. 'That'll get things off with a bang.' 'She knows we're slipping out of her clutches and she's panicking,' commented a working-class man of thirty-six. Radio Forth organized a Silver Jubilee Poetry Competi-

tion. The standard was abysmal, one of the better entries
in terms of rhyme or scansion read:

> Nae Elizabeth the ane,
> Nae Lilabet the twa,
> We'll make our land republican
> When Scotland breaks awa!

Letters in the *Scotsman*[6] denounced the use of the English
coat of arms on the royal car, the St George on its radiator,
the English quarterings on the royal standard and the English
form of the royal arms over the Queen's dais at the Beating of
Retreat.

'I don't know what all the fuss is about,' wrote a working-
class woman of sixty from Glasgow. 'She's the Queen of
Scotland, too, isn't she?' For every republican voice in
Scotland there seemed ten who criticized the Jubilee only
because it did not give proper weight to Scotland's special
status. Polls over the years have consistently shown less
support for the monarchy in Scotland than elsewhere in
the British Isles but have never indicated that the difference
was great. There was nothing in the Queen's reception at
Glasgow, or for that matter in the other Scottish cities, to
indicate that things had radically changed. Except perhaps
in Edinburgh the royal presence worked its magic. Yet it is
possible to detect an indifference far more widespread than
in England, a feeling that the monarch is an irrelevance,
something alien to what matters to Scotland today: that
Elizabeth is, in fact, Elizabeth II, Queen of England.

To anyone who had studied the Coronations of 1937 and
1953 the Jubilee of 1977 held few surprises. Initial apathy,
complaints about expense and wasted effort, a gradual
involvement of the people, hectic turmoil in the final weeks
and then extravaganza was the common pattern of all three
occasions. The only surprise, perhaps, was that there was no
surprise. So much seemed to have changed, there were so

many cogent reasons to expect the Jubilee to be but a pallid reminder of the great royal fiestas of the past: yet when it came to the point all was as it should have been.

Has nothing changed, then? Have the feelings of the British in no way modified over the last forty years?

CHAPTER TEN

To the Future

Three great royal festivals provide beginning, middle and end to the span of time covered by this book. It is only proper that they should do so, for in general the British public rarely thinks about its monarchy except when circumstances draw it to their attention. Coronations, Jubilees and State funerals are pre-eminent examples of such occasions; royal engagements or rumoured engagements, sporting achievements, a speech less than characteristically bland, the promise of a scandal: all of these thrust the royal family into the forefront of the public consciousness. Failing such stimuli, they do not bulk large. In moments of great triumph or tragedy no one turns to Buckingham Palace for comfort or encouragement. Who asked the Queen's opinion of the attack on Suez? Who appealed to George V to take a line on the General Strike? Who cares whether the Duke of Edinburgh feels Knott and Underwood should still play in the English cricket team? On the latter point, at least, it is in fact probable that a great many people would be curious to know the Duke's view, yet it is inherent in the present role of the royal family that he should shrink from committing himself on a subject so sensitive.

The more controversial a subject, the more important – indeed, the more certain – it is that the Queen will refrain from expressing any opinion. When she recently suggested in the most moderate terms that it would be a pity if Great Britain were to disintegrate her words were acclaimed or deplored as if she had propounded something daring and unexpected. It was unexpected, but only because it came from her and was voiced in such a way as to suggest that she actually herself believed in what she was saying and was not merely mouthing the words of her prime minister. On controversial issues the monarch is not expected to comment, in most national events she plays no part. At the end of the last war the crowds flocked to Buckingham Palace to celebrate; but on what other non-royal occasion has the Palace been the centre for rejoicing, or for that matter angry demonstration? If there is a focal point for such assembly it is Trafalgar Square, or perhaps Downing Street. The royal family is irrelevant to nine-tenths of the events that disturb the British people. One of the more remarkable features of Mass Observation's coverage of the two Coronations and the Jubilee is the way in which nobody talked about them at all until a few months before the event. Football was discussed, the Test match, the cost of living, strikes, the weather, yet it took the most arrant coaxing from the Observers to elicit any comment about the royal family.

If one contrasts this apparent indifference with the frenzy prevailing at the time of royal fiesta it is natural that one should feel a certain scepticism. Two questions above all arise to which some answer must be given if the popular enthusiasm at, for instance, the time of the 1977 Jubilee is to be given its proper weight. First, does the rejoicing spring from genuine enthusiasm for the monarchy or from other sources, principally a determination to celebrate something or other if only given half a chance? Second, in so far as the enthusiasm *is* related to the monarchy, is it in existence, even if lying latent, at all times, or is it a short-lived phenomenon, having little to do with the permanent feelings of the people? To both these questions some hints of an answer are given in the previous pages.

As to the first, it is indisputable that the British people enjoys a party. Celebrations do not necessarily betoken zeal for the cause which provokes them. To keep Christmas does not prove that one is a Christian. This book is dotted with examples of people who admitted freely that coronation or jubilee were only excuses for achieving something they had long meant to achieve or for diverting themselves by having a get-together with their friends.

But this is far indeed from being the whole story. Whatever the rationale of the participants it is impossible to conceive any other type of event which would have stimulated the same degree of activity, spread over so long a period and participated in by so many different kinds of people. Conceive the ultimate in conquering heroes; an English football team, for example, which had won the World Cup and stopped over on the way home to rescue a few children from death by fire or drowning. Hysteria would no doubt mount, cheering crowds might line the Mall as they drove in motorcade to take luncheon with their sovereign. Yet it is impossible to believe that even such champions, fresh returned from putting the 'great' back into Great Britain, would stimulate such *nationwide* enthusiasm, let alone a readiness to devote weeks or months of hard work to organizing the celebrations. Any other stimulus might activate one section of the community, perhaps even several sections, but nothing else could so stir the community as a whole.

Nor is it possible to conceive that any other individual would attract the sort of personal devotion and loyalty shown to the Queen. If the Prime Minister were to drive in state from Downing Street to St Paul's, be the occasion never so important nor his equipage so glittering, it is inconceivable that thousands of people would sleep in the street through a cold and rainy night in order to glimpse him as he rode by. Mick Jagger or Rod Stewart would be more likely to command such fervour, yet this support would be limited to a narrow base of predominantly teenage fans; they would never draw into the streets old, middle-aged and young, rich and poor, the extraordinary cross-section of people that composes a royal crowd. There is no other force sufficiently potent to stimulate the British people into behaviour so uncharacteristic, whether in terms of individual sacrifice or co-operative effort, save perhaps some dire emergency which threatened national extinction.

But are these explosions of loyal inebriety, occurring at lengthy intervals, no more than ephemeral phenomena, representing no deep-seated or permanent feeling? Here again it is easy to belittle the significance of coronation and jubilee. As has already been said, between times the public takes its monarchy for granted, the euphoria dies down, the national anthem becomes once more an irritating irrelevance, delaying the start of the news bulletin on royal birthdays. And yet such indifference is never more than superficial; time and again it is shown how a royal engagement, death or scandal will quickly fan the smouldering public interest into a raging fury. Prurient interest in royal gossip is hardly a proof of loyalty, and it is hard to prove that there is more to it than that; yet the immense good-will and fervour released, for instance, by the marriage of Princess Anne, surely shows that enthusiasm for the monarchy is never more than dormant, and in a fitful and shallow sleep at that. It does not take flamboyant pageantry to awaken it. Conceive the possibility of some prime minister announcing that, a few weeks ahead, there would be a referendum on the proposal that Britain should become a republic. Can anyone seriously doubt that those weeks would be dominated by the thunderous roaring of the royalists, that every other issue would be forced into the background and that, on the appointed day, between 85 and 90% of Britain's electorate would prove by their votes what they had demonstrated by their cheers in 1937, 1953 and 1977?

To some extent this popular support would be founded on approval of the present Queen. It was striking in 1977 how many tributes were paid to her conscientiousness and dignity, to the way in which she embodied qualities such as decency, respectability, familial loyalty, which were often represented as being out of fashion but were still cherished by the great mass of her people. And yet the enthusiasm was no less great in 1953 when the Queen's personal qualities were still largely to be established. The speed with which Edward VIII was forgotten showed that, though the individual monarch could play an important role, the institution of monarchy was stronger than any one of its practitioners. Of course a thoroughly bad king or queen could do serious, perhaps even irreparable damage to the throne, but he would have to work hard at it. Mere failure to shine would not be enough. There is a latent force, a power of attraction, in the contemporary monarchy which would survive much indifferent management before it was totally eroded.

To establish the existence of such a force is one thing, to analyse it another. One is back again with Max Weber's 'powerful, magnetic appeal . . . to which men are somehow peacefully and affectionately drawn'. Such an appeal is no more susceptible to precise analysis than concepts such as 'charm' or 'sex appeal'. Because it is attached to an institution rather than an individual, however, it is possible to establish certain constant features which recur throughout the ages. Two elements above all predominate in the nation's enthusiasm for the monarchy and, at the risk of being accused of over-simplification, I would suggest that they underlie every shadow of opinion.

The first is the appeal of the institution to the conservative instincts of most of the British people of every political persuasion. The royal family is at the least a symbol, at the most a guarantee of stability, security, continuity – the preservation of traditional values. It is considered a defence against extremism, against the erosion of family life, against the disintegration of society. Of the positive arguments put forward by those of Mr Hamilton's correspondents who supported the monarchy the most frequently advanced was that the constitutional monarchy was a bulwark against dictatorship, whether of left or right. In the royal service was to be found patriotism and national unity; by her example the Queen encouraged conscientiousness, industry, decency; the monarchy provided a rudder which kept the ship of State stable and sailing in the right direction.

The second, superficially dissimilar yet by no means incompatible element is the appeal to the romantic. At the lowest these are the delights of colourful pageantry and soap-box opera, at a higher level the sense of history incarnate, of the blood royal flowing down through generation after generation from the mists of antiquity. It calls for the most trenchant radicalism or peculiar insensitivity not to feel some thrill of excitement at the extraordinary link with the past which the royal family and their way of life represent. They are but flesh and blood yet to all but a few of even the most sophisticated of their subjects some slight flavour of the supernatural hangs around their lives. No one would deny that Bloch was right when he spoke of the 'deep-down shattering of faith in the supernatural character of royalty' which occurred during the Middle Ages, yet though we know that the Queen eats, drinks and otherwise conducts her physical life upon lines very similar to our own the obstinate conviction lingers on. She is not quite like us.

It would be possible to divide and subdivide these two broad headings into endless subtler categories. No one who has read the preceding pages with even cursory attention can doubt the infinite diversity of the British citizen's response to his monarch. The twin appeals of stability and of romance remain, however, the two umbrellas under which almost all the other elements can be grouped. It does not appear that their potency is seriously waning. Many who thought they were doing so have revised their opinion as a result of the happenings of 1977. It is possible to conceive circumstances – a nuclear bombardment, a Communist take-over – in which the monarchy would abruptly vanish. So also would society as we know it in these islands. Short of some such cataclysm it is hard to believe that the royal family will be in serious threat in the lifetime of any reader of this book.

It would, however, be perfectly possible to destroy those assets which today ensure its continuation. A modernist monarch, noisily pioneering new techniques in sexual liberation, sending the royal children to communes, identifying himself with the most radical elements in national politics, would quickly destroy his conservative appeal. There is plenty of room for the assertive innovator in British society, but Buckingham Palace cannot be his proper habitat. Similarly, a king determined to destroy what is left of the mystique of the Crown, to bring the royal family into the market place, to turn the palaces into office blocks and live in terraced houses, to abandon the Life Guards and the carriages, to travel by bus and bicycle, would soon destroy the romantic appeal of the monarchy. The titular chief of a drab bureaucracy may perform an estimable function, but he will not be a king as desired by the British people.

Is all then for the best in the best of possible worlds? Should the royal family carry on doing precisely what it is doing now and concentrate its efforts on holding on to what it possesses, whether in terms of property, privilege or power? Things are, of course, not as simple as that. The monarchy cannot afford to appear too reactionary, to resist every innovation, to cling to outworn rituals even when they have become inconvenient and unattractive to the British people. The maintenance of a certain grandeur in their life-style must not leave them too far open to charges of extravagance and ostentation. Nor can they be too tepid, too unadventurous. There must be moderation in all things, even in moderation.

As a blueprint for future conduct such qualified counsel may reasonably be felt a little vague. One very general conclusion does, however, seem to emerge from the welter of miscellaneous evidence. There is as great a risk in reform as there is in standing still, perhaps even a greater risk. Change for the sake of change is not merely pointless but dangerous. The British people do not want any *fundamental* changes in the way the royal family conducts its life. Kings or queens must concern themselves with the facts of contemporary life, understand the issues, encourage new departures. It is right that the Prince of Wales should fly jets, revel in technological innovations. But he must not accommodate himself slavishly to fashion, otherwise, when the fashion changes, he will find himself out of favour. Any proposal for a drastic alteration in his appearance or behaviour should be looked at with caution, and then looked at again.

If we leave out of account, therefore, the possibility of national disaster or some wild urge to self-destruction on the part of our monarchs, it seems that the institution is secure. The Queen has already demonstrated that the future is safe in her hands, and everything which is publicly known about the Prince of Wales suggests that he will be equally capable of managing affairs. This assumes that the Prince of Wales will in due course succeed. It is significant that the two great triumphs of monarchy have been the Jubilee of King George V and the Coronation of Queen Elizabeth. The first was the apotheosis of a beloved father-figure, the second the victory of youth and hope. Together they confirm what is anyway evident from the evidence of this book; that the British people like their monarchs old, wise and paternal, or young and hopeful. The Queen's stature will grow steadily as she advances through the arduous middle years to revered longevity. Those who suggest that she should abdicate misunderstand the appeal of royalty. It matters little that the Queen should be less agile, slower to read State papers, a more reluctant opener of hospitals or launcher of ships; what is important is that she should still be there, in noble antiquity, a link with the past, the fount of wisdom – real or fancied – based on infinite experience. In the end to hand on the Crown to a grandson of twenty-odd would be the ideal formula for the perpetuation of the monarchy. The Golden Jubilee of 2002 might be a suitable occasion.

This would, of course, require the premature disappearance of the Prince of Wales; a step the need for which he might reasonably consider inadequately proven. It would also assume that the future incumbent would be as talented

'Cheer up sunshine, sleeping through the lot isn't so
bad, there's always the Golden Jubilee in year 2002.'

and conscientious as the present Prince shows every sign
of being. It is anyway a counsel of perfection; the monarchy
will survive quite happily without any juggling with the
succession. It will survive because the vast majority of the
British people feel a need for it; at the weakest would mildly
regret its disappearance, at the strongest feel passionately
that it is a vital part not only of the national life but of their
own personal existence. Republicanism has failed to grow
over the last twenty-five years, when so much seemed pro-
pitious for its rapid increase. I can see no reason why it

should do better in the next twenty-five.

I cannot but feel this is a conclusion at which we should rejoice. I am no more intemperate a royalist than when I began this study, but I am far more firmly convinced that the British want the royal family, that their reasons for doing so are sensible, even meritorious, and that our national life would be impoverished if the monarchy were to be eliminated. It seems right to end not with a purple passage but with this muted trumpet blast.

'Ten Years of Listen and Look'

The following summary of Mass Observation was issued in their Bulletin *in February 1947.*

Just ten years ago, on 12 February 1937, the first thirty Mass Observers, nucleus of the present 2000-strong National Panel, made the first Mass Observation experiment. MO began when thirty people who had never met, who lived in widely scattered parts of the country, and who held widely different views on life, agreed to write down in detail all that happened to them on one arbitrarily chosen day of their lives.

At about the same time half a dozen people who had given up their ordinary jobs for the purpose went to live in a Lancashire cotton town ('Worktown') to make a whole-time study of human activity there. A parallel survey was started at Blackpool where most 'Worktowners' spend their holidays.

Right from the start, Mass Observation has worked on this dual system of collecting information. A full-time staff of trained investigators keep an objective record of mass behaviour in all its aspects; while a self-elected part-time voluntary staff keep the individual record, especially the record of subjective attitude and private outlook.

Our tenth anniversary is an occasion for reviewing the past and clarifying MO's function in the future. What does

Mass Observation mean? The simplest answer is that it means observation *of* the masses. But another and important part of its meaning is observation *by* the masses, of themselves and their environment. This aspect of MO brings into focus its particular divergencies from other organizations.

Words

The study of human beings differs from the study of all other objects in one simple fundamental respect. Human beings talk. What they say or write is a vitally important part of their behaviour which can not only explain their own motivations, fulfilments, and frustrations, but can influence the behaviour of others. A great part of Mass Observation's job is necessarily the study of words spoken and words written.

Words, notoriously, can be used to conceal or to reveal, to lead or to mislead. If words are to be used to explain human behaviour and not to explain it away, the context in which they are spoken must always be taken into consideration. Except on subjects about which they feel very strongly, what people *say* is adapted and varied to suit their audience, and bears a relationship to what they *think*, *feel*, and *believe* which can only be assessed from a knowledge of their relationship to the person, or people, to whom they are talking. Even if feelings are exceedingly strong, it is only when taken off their guard that the majority of people will say *all* that is in their mind before a stranger.

Professor Malinowski, discussing Mass Observation in its first published work said: 'In human affairs the more subjective the behaviour, the more objective are the scientific data which it furnishes.' In simple terms of action and reaction this means that what people do and say during an air-raid is a more reliable clue to their real nature than what they do and say in a drawing-room, where their pattern of behaviour is mapped out in advance, and where (apart from the task of keeping within the expected pattern) they are not so subjectively involved.

In terms of words written and words spoken the statement implies:

1. That words only provide useful information about the person using them to the extent to which that person is 'interested' and 'involved' in the subject about which he is speaking. To quote Prof. Malinowski again: 'Ask your informant questions which do not affect him and you will receive rambling irrelevant divagations. But touch him on the raw; release some of his dominant interests or passions; above all make it clear to him that upon what he answers some practical consequences may depend – in short that in this verbal statement he carries out a significant and relevant act – then and then only you will receive answers which are genuine scientific documents.'

2. Secondly, and by implication from the above, that the informant must not only be indulging in subjective behaviour when he speaks for his words to provide objective data, but that the situation in which he finds himself must be such as to encourage him to speak 'the truth'. A person striving to conceal attitudes which he holds strongly is indulging in intensively subjective behaviour, but his words do not provide objective data.

Say and Do

These few, and still not fully studied, principles explain some of the reasons why Mass Observation adopts the techniques, incomplete though they may be, which are now associated with its name. When we are collecting verbal data our aim is not *simply* to record what people say, but to evaluate what they say in relation to the context in which they say it. We aim – often unsuccessfully – at recording those verbal statements which are 'significant and relevant acts', and *relating* these statements to the general climate of top-

level talk and socially accepted attitude; and finally at
relating these different levels of *saying* to actual physical
behaviour – the level of *doing*.

In anthropological work the person who provides the
anthropologist with verbal documentation is called an
'informant'. In 'social survey' work the person who provides
the documentation is usually called a 'respondent'. The
distinction between providing *information*, and providing
merely a *response* or *reply*, is one which, for many years,
Mass Observation has been seeking to clarify and bring
to the notice of those engaged in this type of research. It is
this distinction which, in our view, makes the formal questionnaire a method of obtaining information which, despite
its many uses, has at present inadequately realized limitations.

The Panel

MO's National Panel has the advantage over other sources
of information that its members have special motives for
telling 'the truth' about themselves, their views, ideas, and
habits.

Firstly, they are aware of, and are interested in, the purpose for which information is collected, and they know that a
mere repetition of the socially acceptable answer to any
questions they may be asked is of no value for this purpose.
Secondly, they are assured of anonymity and know that
nothing they write will in any way reflect on them personally.
Even if published, it will be so cut as to be completely
unidentifiable. In ten years we have used the records of
thousands of observers, and we have never let an observer
down.

The importance of this second factor can be seen from an
example. Suppose that a person has for many years supported
a particular political party, and his views on politics are now
becoming a little less secure. He is, as yet, very far from
changing his political affiliation but he is not so sure as he
was about the party he still backs. In private conversation

with trusted friends, he may perhaps confess his doubts; though, if the friends are not openly critical as well, he may well tone his views down or express them in an apologetic way. In conversation with an ardent member of the opposing party, he will very likely hide his doubts under an increasingly arduous protestation of the rightness of *his* party's cause. If he is visited by a stranger with a questionnaire, it is unlikely that he will express criticisms which he feels are disloyal to the party. If, on the other hand, he is able to record his views *anonymously* and to submit the record to some dispassionate body or individual who he knows will neither make political capital out of it, nor feel that it reflects either on his loyalty or his consistency, he has no reason for concealing what is in his mind.

Private Opinion and Public Opinion

Elsewhere we have described public opinion as the opinion which people are willing to express *in public* to a stranger. Anyone who cares to examine his own *private* opinion on a number of subjects will quickly see that it often differs markedly from his *public* opinion on the same subjects. But opinion is only the top, most rational, layer of the whole complex of feeling, emotion, fear, hope, and finally of unconscious driving force, which determines a person's attitude and behaviour. Public opinion may serve as a disguise for private opinion, but private opinion is often itself a compromise with *feelings* which have not yet had time to translate themselves into opinion at all.

When a sudden shift in public opinion takes place, it is, in Mass Observation's experience, a reflection of a change in *private* opinion which has been carrying on slowly and steadily over a period. Thus an outbreak of anti-American public opinion followed the end of the war, but anti-American *private* opinion had been maturing over a long period. Publicly expressed criticism of Russian policy appeared suddenly during the early days of UNO, but privately expressed uneasiness had been apparent some considerable time before the end of the war. In Britain, public opinion generally changes when *published* opinion (in press and radio) and *leader* opinion (in parliament and pulpit) lifts the social sanction on public expression. But private opinion must have changed first – or been gradually led – otherwise press, radio, politician and parson have nothing to work on. The 1945 election campaign was an example of an all-out attempt to influence public opinion which failed because private opinion was firmly set in a different groove. Through a study of private opinion, MO was able to say with conviction what the result of the election would be many months before it took place.

Thus changes in public opinion naturally *follow* changes in private opinion, and private opinion follows changes in feeling and emotion.

Formal questionnaires measure the top level of public opinion – the stranger-to-stranger level of socially acceptable talk. While a questionnaire can be invaluable in providing an indication of the social atmosphere of the moment, MO tries to get below this level and to find out about the meaning and implications of public opinion, and its likely future directions, through an examination of its sources in private opinion, feelings and underlying emotional attitudes. The value of the Panel lies in a relationship which enables its members to write about these deeper levels which they recognize in themselves, but about which they, like anyone else, would be unwilling to talk in detail to a strange interviewer, or, often, to their own personal friends.

Fieldwork

The methods we adopt in the fieldwork studies by our whole-time staff arise from the same source. We use questionnaires to obtain an idea of the general social atmosphere. Thus, in our book *Britain and her Birthrate* quite extensive use was made of a questionnaire. The results told us a great deal about the sort of social talk which is going about the desirability or otherwise of having large families. They mapped out the atmosphere of respectable argument. But the results of asking married women *why* they did not have more babies, and what they thought might encourage them to have more, needed the strongest possible qualification and explanation in order to avoid the impression that what these women *said* was their reason for having small families was *in fact* the direct and basic reason for their behaviour.

Whenever it is technically possible, therefore, MO places its whole-time investigators right inside the environments concerned in any survey. Here they record what is done and said, without any prompting or question-asking of the people they are observing. Such techniques are not always feasible. When they are not, MO still places great importance on the *relationship* between investigator and investigated. On the nature of this relationship depends the interpretation which can be placed on the data collected. In the case of the National Panel of voluntary observers, the relationship is based on a realization of the purpose for which information is being sought. This gives the Panel its unique value.

These are some of the principles. The National Panel is a vital part of the fact-finding machinery. It is not a cross-section of the nation – no group of intelligible correspondent reporters could be. It consists of a large number of people of widely differing backgrounds, with different views on any, and every, subject, *who are willing to talk with the brake off*. A statistical cross-section can only be approached under conditions which make them talk with the brake *on*. A statistically based analysis of the 'respectable' accepted attitude remains evasive however elaborate the steps taken to ensure that the sources from which it is collected are representative. In all Mass Observation's work our primary object is to ensure the *subjective validity* of the material we collect.

TOM HARRISSON

Notes

CHAPTER ONE: The Crown in History

1. Marc Bloch. *The Royal Touch*. London, 1973. p. 3.
2. Jeremy Collier. *Ecclesiastical History of Great Britain*. 1840. Vol. 1. p. 532.
3. Sheila Macdonald. 'Old-world Survivals in Ross-shire'. *Folklore*. 1903. Vol. 14.
4. Herbert Spencer. *The Principles of Sociology*. London, 1969 edition, Part II, Chapter I, p. 164.
5. 'The Psychology of Contemporary Monarchy'. *New Statesman*. 1 February 1936. pp. 141–2.
6. Max Weber. *Essays in Sociology*. London, 1948.
7. Ernest Barker. *The Character of Britain*. Oxford, 1950. p. 10.
8. 'The Psychology of Contemporary Monarchy'. *New Statesman*. 1 February 1936.
9. H. H. Gerth & C. Wright Mills (Ed.). *From Max Weber*. London, 1948. p. 264.
10. Harold Nicolson. *King George V*. London, 1952. p. 308.
11. 'The Psychology of Contemporary Monarchy'. *New Statesman*. 1 February 1936.
12. Christopher Hibbert. *Edward VII*. London, 1976. p. 107.
13. Philip Magnus. *King Edward VII*. London, 1964. p. 101.
14. Christopher Hibbert. *Edward VII*. London, 1976. p. 73.
15. Rudyard Kipling. 'The Widow at Windsor'. *Collected Verse*. London, 1940. p. 413.
16. G. E. Buckle (Ed.). *The Letters of Queen Victoria*. Third Series. Vol. III. p. 174.
17. Elizabeth Longford. *Victoria R.I.* London, 1964. p. 548.
18. H. G. Wells. *Experiment in Autobiography*. London, 1934. Vol. 1.
19. Christopher Hibbert. *Edward VII*. London, 1976. p. 60.
20. ibid., p. 64.
21. Munby. cit. Christopher Hibbert. *Edward VII*. London, 1976. p. 116.
22. Philip Magnus. *King Edward VII*. London, 1964. p. 297.
23. ibid., p. 429.
24. Kingsley Martin. *The Crown and the Establishment*. London, 1962. p. 68.
25. Harold Nicolson. *King George V*. London, 1952. p. 86.

26. ibid., p. 196.
27. Leonard Harris. *Long to Reign Over Us?* London, 1966. p. 132.
28. *War Memoirs*. London, 1934. Vol. 4. p. 1961.
29. Leonard Harris. *Long to Reign Over Us?* p. 132.
30. Harold Nicolson. *King George V.* p. 308.
31. ibid., p. 526.
32. John Wheeler-Bennett. *King George VI.* London, 1958. p. 263.
33. Kingsley Martin. *The Crown and the Establishment.* London, 1962. p. 22.
34. Bolitho. *Edward VII.* p. 210.
35. Leonard Harris. *Long to Reign Over Us?* p. 132.
36. Sir Charles Petrie. *The Modern British Monarchy.* London, 1961. p. 176.
37. Harold Nicolson. *Diaries and Letters 1930–1939.* London, 1966. p. 280.
38. Leonard Harris. *Long to Reign Over Us?* p. 43.
39. Harold Nicolson. *King George V.* p. 247.
40. ibid., p. 281.
41. MO Archive. Box 494. File 2641.
42. John Wheeler-Bennett. *King George VI.* p. 298.
43. ibid., p. 299.
44. Dorothy Laird. *Queen Elizabeth the Queen Mother.* London, 1966. p. 155.
45. Warren Bradley Wells. *Why Edward Went.* New York, 1937. pp. 3-4.
46. John Wheeler-Bennett. *King George VI.* p. 247.
47. Dermot Morrah. *To Be A King.* London, 1968. p. 21.

CHAPTER TWO: Coronation, 1937

1. P. E. Schramm. *A History of the English Coronation.* London, 1937. p. 1.
2. Margaret Lane. *New Statesman.* 6 May 1953.
3. Robert Bocock. *Ritual in Industrial Society.* London, 1974. p. 105. cf. E. Durkheim. *The Elementary Forms of the Religious Life.* New York, 1961.
4. Edward Shils & Michael Young. 'The Meaning of the Coronation'. N. Birnbaum. 'Monarchs and Sociologists. A reply to Professor Shils and Mr Young'. *Sociological Review.* 1953. Vol. 1. No. 1. and 1955. Vol. 3. No. 1.
5. Bronislaw Malinowski. 'A nation-wide intelligence service'. *First Year's Work.* London, 1938. p. 114.
6. Statistics from the Mass Observation Archive for the 1953 Coronation (Box Cor: 7).
7. Unless otherwise stated the material in the rest of this chapter

comes either from the Mass Observation Archive or the MO study of the Coronation, *May the Twelfth* (London, 1937). Most material is to be found in original in the Archive, but some is missing and some material actually in the Archive was not used in the book.

CHAPTER THREE: The Monarchy at War

1. Mass Observation Diaries, Misc.
2. ibid., 1/2.
3. ibid., 6/10.
4. ibid., 16/18.
5. Richard Rose & Dennis Kavanagh. *The Monarchy in Contemporary British Culture. Comparative Politics*, July 1976. Vol. 8, No. 4. p. 30.
6. Mass Observation Diaries, FR 247. 4 July 1940.
7. Mass Observation Diaries, 20/25.
8. Bernard Knowles. *Southampton: The English Gateway*. Southampton, 1951. p. 148.
9. Tom Harrisson. *Living Through the Blitz*. London, 1976. p. 164.
10. Mass Observation Diaries, 13.
11. John Wheeler-Bennett. *King George VI*. p. 469.
12. Mass Observation Diaries, FR 247.
13. ibid.
14. ibid.
15. Mass Observation Diaries, Misc.
16. John Wheeler-Bennett. *King George VI*. p. 467.
17. Dorothy Laird. *Queen Elizabeth the Queen Mother*. London, 1966. p. 217.
18. Mass Observation Diaries, Misc.
19. Mass Observation Diaries, 17 November 1940. cit. John Wheeler-Bennett. *King George VI*. p. 467.
20. Mass Observation Diaries, 12.

CHAPTER FOUR: Wedding and Funeral

1. News Quota. 15 May 1947.
2. News Quota. 12 October 1947.
3. Basil Boothroyd. *Philip, An Informal Biography*. London, 1971. p. 28.
4. ibid. p. 33.
5. News Quota. 14 July and 12 October 1947.
6. Gallup. 5 November 1947.

CHAPTER FIVE: Coronation, 1953

1. Mass Observation 1953 Coronation Material. Box 7. Unless otherwise stated all material in this chapter is drawn from the ten boxes in this series, the most substantial reports by Mass Observers being found in Box 7.
2. *News Chronicle*, 21 May 1953.
3. Mass Observation First National Survey. 1000 people questioned.
4. Mass Observation London Survey. 12 May 1953.
5. Tom Harrisson. *Britain Revisited*. London, 1961. p. 237.
6. *Daily Sketch*, 8 June 1953.
7. *New Statesman*. 29 May 1953.
8. *Portsmouth Evening News*. 1 June 1953.
9. Harold Nicolson. *Diaries and Letters 1945–1962*. London, 1968. p. 230.
10. *Willesden Chronicle*, 12 June 1953.
11. Kingsley Martin. *The Crown and the Establishment*. p. 119.

CHAPTER SIX: The Democratization of the Royal Family

1. It has proved impossible to verify the sources of all these figures, and their statistical value no doubt also varies widely. 1956, Mass Observation Survey (Tom Harrisson. *Britain Revisited*. London, 1961. p. 231); 1958, Mass Observation Survey 627; 1960, Mass Observation Survey (Leonard Harris. *Long to Reign Over Us?* London, 1966. p. 77); 1964, ibid.; 9–14 July 1969, NOP; October 1969, NOP (Special Supplement II) and *Daily Mirror*, 17 October 1969; 8–14 June 1971, NOP; 6–9 January 1972, Gallup; May 1973, Gallup; 11–16 February 1976, Gallup; 6–10 May 1976, Gallup.
2. Mass Observation Diaries, Misc.
3. Mass Observation Diaries, Misc.
4. BIP Survey No. 451A.
5. *The National and English Review*, September 1957. Vol. 149. No. 895.
6. Robert Lacey. *Majesty*. London, 1977. p. 255.
7. Jeremy Murray-Brown (Ed.). *The Monarchy and its Future*. London, 1969. p. 51.
8. *Daily Mail*, 12 August 1957.
9. Leonard Harris. *Long to Reign Over Us?* p. 104.
10. ibid., p. 214.
11. William Hamilton. *My Queen and I*. London, 1975, p. 28.
12. BBC Audience Research Report (VR/69/375). October 1969.
13. NOP. 9–14 July 1969.
14. *The Listener*, 26 June 1969.
15. J. G. Blumler, J. R. Brown, A. J. Ewbank & T. J. Nossiter. 'Attitudes to the Monarchy: Their Structure and Development during a

Ceremonial Occasion'. *Political Studies*. Vol. 19. No. 2. June 1971.
16. NOP. 9–14 July 1969.
17. NOP. Special Survey II, 31 October–1 November 1969.

CHAPTER EIGHT: The Forgotten Family?

1. Harold Nicolson. *Monarchy*. London, 1962. p. 303.
2. *Daily Express*, 3 November 1968.
3. Mass Observation Poll. cit. Leonard Harris. *Long to Reign Over Us?* p. 62. Unless otherwise stated the quotations that follow come also from this work.
4. Hamilton Correspondence. 10 January 1975.
5. Social and Community Planning Research Poll. 17 October 1969.
6. 'Working-Class Conservatives'. *British Journal of Sociology*. 1967. Vol. 18. p. 280.
7. Richard Rose & Dennis Kavanagh. 'The Monarchy in Contemporary British Culture'. *Op. cit.*
8. Richard Hoggart. *The Uses of Literacy*. London, 1957. pp. 92–3.
9. Gallup. January 1963; June 1968; December 1968; June 1969; May 1973; November 1975.
10. Richard Hoggart. *The Uses of Literacy*. p. 93.
11. Richard Rose & Dennis Kavanagh. 'The Monarchy in Contemporary British Culture'.
12. Tom Harrisson. *Britain Revisited*. London, 1961. p. 231.
13. Jeremy Murray-Brown (Ed.). *The Monarchy and its Future*. London, 1969. pp. 189-90.
14. Richard Rose & Dennis Kavanagh. 'The Monarchy in Contemporary British Culture'. *Comparative Politics*. July 1976. Vol. 8. No. 4.
15. 'Face the Press'. Tyne-Tees Television. 20 March 1968.
16. Brian Masters. *Dreams about HM The Queen*. London, 1972.
17. Mass Observation Diaries, Box 8, File 5.
18. Dorothy Laird. *Queen Elizabeth the Queen Mother*. London, 1966. p. 293.
19. William Hamilton. *My Queen and I*. p. 140.
20. Basil Boothroyd. *Philip. An Informal Biography*. London, 1971. p. 224.

CHAPTER NINE: Jubilee, 1977

Unless otherwise stated all quotations come from the Mass Observation Archive, which is provisionally sorted according to the sex and identity of the Observer, but not yet properly catalogued.

1. *The Bingley Guardian*, 18 March 1977.

2. *Sheerness Times Guardian.* 12 April 1977.
3. *Eastern Daily Press*, 26 May 1977.
4. *West Highland Free Press*, 14 May 1977.
5. *The Times*, 5 June 1977.
6. *Scotsman*, 27 May 1977.

Index